The

Bernese Mountain Dog

An Owner's Guide To

A HAPPY HEALTHY PET

Howell Book House

Wiley Publishing, Inc.

Book Design: Michele Laseau
Cover Design: Iris Jeromnimon
External Features Illustration by Shelley Norris
Other Illustrations by Jeff Yesh
  All photography by Mary Bloom unless otherwise noted.
  Joan Balzarini: 96
  Mary Bloom: 96, 136, 145
  Paulette Braun/Pets by Paulette: 96
  Buckinghambill American Cocker Spaniels: 148
  Sian Cox: 134
  Dr. Ian Dunbar: 98, 101, 103, 111, 116–117, 122, 123, 127
  Dan Lyons: 96
  Cathy Merrithew: 129
  Liz Palika: 133
  Susan Rezy: 96–97
  Judith Strom: 96, 107, 110, 128, 130, 135, 137, 139, 140, 144, 149, 150
Production Team: M. Faunette Johnston, Angel Perez, and Heather Pope

Contents

Welcome
to the
World
of the

part one

Bernese
Mountain Dog

External Features of the Bernese Mountain Dog

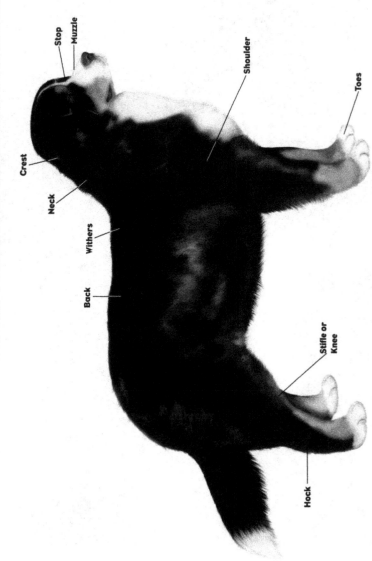

- Stop
- Muzzle
- Shoulder
- Toes
- Crest
- Neck
- Withers
- Back
- Stifle or Knee
- Hock

chapter 1

What Is a **Bernese Mountain Dog?**

The Bernese Mountain Dog attracts attention wherever he goes. A stroll with one of these dogs is often a stop and go session. Everyone you meet will inquire about what kind of dog he is or will jubilantly recognize the breed. With a wagging tail and quick glance for his owner's approval of time-out, a typical Bernese Mountain Dog will greet each person as eagerly as a new star signing autographs. His greatest joy, however, is when a child wants to meet him. There is an almost magical bond between children and Bernese Mountain Dogs.

Absolutely striking in his appearance, the Bernese Mountain Dog is unforgettably beautiful. The vivid, rich black, rust, and white coloration in a pattern of classic markings is the hall-mark of the breed. Those unfamiliar with Bernese often venture to guess on seeing their first, "Is it a black St. Bernard?" When told no and given the name, Bernese Mountain Dog, they frequently repeat it as Burmese, confusing the name with that of the cat which originated in Burma. Bernese Mountain Dogs trace their roots to the Alpine setting of the Canton of Bern in Switzerland. There, they developed as versatile farm dogs, capable of driving livestock, pulling carts, protecting property, and providing companionship. Centuries of such service have produced a remarkable working dog with a keen desire to please and to be with people as the family dog.

It is easy to see why Berners have such a devoted following.

Discovering Bernese Mountain Dogs

The captivating beauty and marvelous temperament of the Bernese Mountain Dog endear him to today's owners, who upon getting to know the breed, wonder why it took them so long to discover it. Proud owners talk enthusiastically about their "Berners," a direct reference to the breed's Swiss name, *Berner Sennenhunde.* Newcomers to the breed find the search for information and chances to meet Berners and their Bernerfolk a rewarding challenge.

Dependent upon geographic location, opportunities to actually see a Bernese Mountain Dog are not always readily available, even at dog shows. For this reason sightings are sometimes as exciting as bird watching. Being highly photogenic, Bernese Mountain Dogs have become quite visible in a variety of advertising media, thus piquing the public's curiousity even further.

Standard of Excellence

To understand any breed, it is essential to become acquainted with the breed's standard as accepted by the American Kennel Club. The definitive profile of the breed standard details the specifications of an ideal specimen and describes the characteristics unique to each breed.

The first Bernese Mountain Dog standard in America was taken from the Swiss standard current at that time. It was adopted in 1937 when the breed was recognized by the American Kennel Club and placed in the Working Group. Each breed's standard is under the guardianship of its parent club thereby enabling those most familiar with a particular breed to make revisions. In 1980 and again in 1990, the Bernese Mountain Dog Club of America, acting in that capacity, proposed revisions to the standard which were voted upon and approved by its nationwide membership prior to submission to the AKC for its approval.

> **THE AMERICAN KENNEL CLUB**
>
> Familiarly referred to as "the AKC," the American Kennel Club is a nonprofit organization devoted to the advancement of purebred dogs. The AKC maintains a registry of recognized breeds and adopts and enforces rules for dog events including shows, obedience trials, field trials, hunting tests, lure coursing, herding, earthdog trials, agility and the Canine Good Citizen program. It is a club of clubs, established in 1884 and composed, today, of over 500 autonomous dog breed clubs throughout the United States. Each club is represented by a delegate; the delegates make up the legislative body of the AKC, voting on rules and electing directors. The AKC maintains the Stud Book—the record of every dog ever registered with the AKC—and publishes a variety of materials on purebred dogs, including a monthly magazine, books and numerous educational pamphlets. For more information, contact the AKC at the address listed in Chapter 13, "Resources," and look for the names of their publications in Chapter 12, "Recommended Reading."

A brief exploration of some of the expectations described in the present standard will serve for better understanding the Bernese Mountain Dog. Quotations from the standard are italicized, and the author's comments follow. To obtain a copy of the official standard, write to the American Kennel Club, 5580 Centerview Drive, Suite 200, Raleigh, NC 27606.

General Appearance

The Bernese Mountain Dog is a striking, tri-colored, large dog. He is sturdy and balanced. He is intelligent, strong and agile enough to do the draft and droving work for which he was used in the mountainous regions of his origin.

This passage describes the total dog. The components creating the Bernese Mountain Dog's striking beauty are his coat and markings in combination with a harmonious blend of strength, size, substantial structure, and impressive demeanor. He must look physically capable of fulfilling the breed's original purpose of pulling loaded carts and driving livestock in the rugged terrain of Switzerland.

Dogs appear masculine, while bitches are distinctly feminine.

While both males and females have the striking characteristics of the breed, males are quite commanding in appearance, having a more massive body, broader head, and heavier coat than females. The majesty of the male is softly mirrored in the female, making it relatively easy to distinguish the sexes. When comparing the overall impression of males and females, it is important to consider age and relative maturity.

Size, Proportion, Substance

Measured at the withers, dogs are 25 to 27½ inches; bitches are 23 to 26 inches. Though appearing square, Bernese Mountain Dogs are slightly longer in body than they are tall. Sturdy bone is of great importance. The body is full.

Height is based upon measurement at the highest point of the shoulders. With the overall range of height being 23 to 27 ½ inches, it is not unusual to see a significant difference in size in a group of male and female Bernese Mountain Dogs. The proportional ratio of height to length is approximately 9:10 which creates the balance referred to in the general appearance section. Again, the word sturdy is used, emphasizing the importance of solid, structural strength. Weight range for males is approximately 80 to 120 pounds and for females, 75 to 100 pounds.

HEAD

Expression is intelligent, animated and gentle.

As with people, the expressions of Bernese Mountain Dogs change with mood, situation and whether alert or at ease. Expressions are best assessed when the dog is at attention, with ears swiveled forward.

The eyes are dark brown and slightly oval in shape with close-fitting eyelids. Inverted or everted eyelids are serious faults. Blue eye color is a disqualification.

The darker the brown eye color, the more desirable it is. Eyelids that turn inward or outward may lead to health problems with the affected eye or eyes. Blue eye color is light, sky blue and easily recognized. It should not be confused with the deep, dark, bluish brown of some young puppies. While blue eyes are not a health concern, they do not portray correct type. Dogs having one or both blue eyes are disqualified in the show ring and should not be used for breeding. Instead, they are fully able to function as pets and may participate in obedience and other events, such as agility.

The official standard describes the Bernese Mountain Dog's expression as intelligent, animated, and gentle.

The ears are medium sized, set high, triangular in shape, gently rounded at the tip, and hang close to the head when in repose. When the Bernese Mountain Dog is alert, the ears are brought forward and raised at the base; the top of the ear is level with the top of the skull.

The ears contribute a great deal to expression. In full-coated, mature adults, long ear-fringe hairs may give the appearance of a fairly long ear. Actually, the bottom of the ear leather is approximately level with the corner of the mouth. Hound-like ears are undesirable.

The skull is flat on top and broad, with a slight furrow and well-defined, but not exaggerated stop. The muzzle is strong and straight.

The slight furrow of the skull is less noticeable in puppies than in adults. This slight, side to side indentation begins above the stop, proceeding upward over the top of the skull, gradually diminishing at the approximate middle of the head.

The muzzle is slightly longer than the skull. Viewed from above, the head is shaped like a blunt-ended wedge. Setter or St. Bernard-like heads do not correctly represent head type.

The nose is always black.

When Bernese Mountain Dog puppies are born, their noses are pink, gradually becoming mottled with gray that darkens to black. It is not unusual to see a puppy having a tiny pink spot or two as late as 5 or 6 months of age.

The lips are clean and, as the Bernese Mountain Dog is a dry-mouthed breed, the flews are only slightly developed.

The greatly valued dry mouth of Bernese Mountain Dogs is the result of the lips being free of excessive, fleshy development. The flews, that portion of the upper lip, particularly toward the corners of the mouth, should be sufficiently tight to be free of droopiness as they curve into the lower jaw.

The teeth meet in a scissors bite. An overshot or undershot bite is a serious fault. Dentition is complete.

The upper front teeth should fit neatly over the lower teeth to form a scissors bite that is preferred. A level bite with upper and lower teeth resting on each other is acceptable. A serious fault occurs when the upper, front teeth extend over the lower front teeth forming a gap (overshot), or when the reverse occurs with the lower teeth extending beyond the upper front teeth (undershot).

Full dentition is represented in the adult dog by 42 teeth, 22 in the lower and 20 in the upper jaws. Missing teeth are only identifiable after the second teeth have come in. Such absence would be one or more premolars, those teeth directly behind the canines on each side of the upper and lower jaws.

NECK, TOPLINE, BODY

*The **neck** is strong, muscular and of medium length. The **topline** is level from the withers to the croup. The **chest** is deep and capacious with well-sprung, but not barrel shaped, ribs and brisket reaching at least to the elbows. The back is broad and firm. The **loin** is strong. The **croup** is broad and firmly rounded to the tail insertion. The **tail** is bushy. It should be carried low when in repose. An upward swirl is permissible when the dog is alert, but the tail may never curl or be carried over the back. The bones in the tail should feel straight and should reach to the hock joint or below. A kink in the tail is a fault.*

The overall impression should be sturdiness and balance represented by a straight back supporting a powerful body with a well-developed chest capable of being harnessed for draft work. Completing the picture is a beautiful, bushy tail, the barometer of a dog's feelings. With the dog in motion, the tail is raised at a slightly upward angle. Sickle and curled tails detract from the free flowing balance that is conveyed in the moving dog. The tail tip should not touch the back.

Forequarters

*The shoulders are moderately laid back, flat-lying, well-muscled and never loose. The **legs** are straight and strong and the **elbows** are well under the shoulder when the dog is standing. The **pasterns** slope very slightly, but are never weak.*

The forequarters provide the pulling assemblage of a draft dog. The structure of the front is greatly dependent upon a properly developed chest. Well-boned legs should be parallel. Feet turning outward or inward create weakness.

Dewclaws may be removed. The feet are round with well-arched toes.

The removal of front dewclaws at about 3 days of age gives a tidy appearance and eliminates the need for frequent trimming, but not all breeders have them removed.

Hindquarters

The thighs are broad, strong and muscular. The stifles are moderately bent and taper smoothly into the hocks. The hocks are well let down and straight as viewed from the rear.

The hindquarters of a draft dog provide push while the front pulls. Like a vehicle with four-wheel drive, the front and rear work in combination. The hind legs should be parallel. Cow hocks, with the hocks turning in, are weak and therefore undesirable.

Dewclaws should be removed. Feet are compact and turn neither in nor out.

Bernese Mountain Dogs are usually born with rear dewclaws. Sometimes they are double. Their removal by a veterinarian at about 3 days of age safeguards the dog from having these appendages get caught or torn.

COAT

The coat is thick, moderately long and slightly wavy or straight. It has a bright natural sheen. Extremely curly or extremely dull-looking coats are undesirable.

The eye-catching mantle of a lustrous, full coat is the finishing touch on these magnificent dogs of the Alps. It is definitely part of their appeal. The natural coat has the remarkable quality of being quite weather resistant and almost self-cleaning in nature, making it easy to keep. There is an undercoat of short dense hair that supports the outercoat.

Puppies start out with a baby-bear soft coat that is gradually replaced with a second, often wavy, coat, particularly on the top of the back. Many times this luxuriant, first year coat has a bit of curl that would make any girl envious. The next coat is almost always much less wavy.

The Bernese Mountain Dog is shown in natural coat and undue trimming is to be discouraged.

The intent of the standard is to preserve the natural appearance of the dog in the show ring, just as it seeks to preserve the physical qualities needed to perform the tasks for which the Bernese Mountain Dog was bred.

In actual practice, most dogs being presented in the ring have been blow-dried with a high velocity jet of air that creates a very handsome, but relatively temporary appearance of having the hair stand out from the body, giving a fuller-coated look. Trimming is carefully crafted for ultimate enhancement without looking trimmed. Extremes in trimming or sculpting the coat negate the desired natural appearance. The ears, hocks, and feet may be trimmed for a neater appearance. The clipping of whiskers is optional.

A lustrous coat is a hallmark of the breed.

COLOR AND MARKINGS

The Bernese Mountain Dog is tri-colored. The ground color is jet black. The markings are rich rust and clear white. Symmetry of markings is desired. Rust appears over each eye, on the cheeks reaching to at least the corner of the mouth, on each side of the chest, on all four legs, and under the tail. There is a white blaze and muzzle band. A white marking on the chest typically forms an inverted cross. The tip of the tail is white. White on the feet is desired but must not extend higher than the pasterns. Markings other than described are to be faulted in direct relationship to the extent of the

13

deviation. White legs or a white collar are serious faults. Any ground color other than black is a disqualification.

The color and distinctive markings, frequently cited as the breed's hallmark, are undeniably breathtaking. Considerable variation in markings can occur, all within the latitude of perfection. Narrow, medium, or wide blaze, the extent of rust on the cheeks, the amount of white on the feet and tail tip, and the shape of the chest markings may vary significantly while remaining correct. These differentiations present an interesting array for selection according to one's preference. Overmarking or undermarking of white and lack of symmetry, dependent upon location and extent, determine the degree of the fault.

One marking of particular interest is the typical inverted cross formation on the chest. This is often called a Swiss Cross in reference to the national banner of Switzerland, a white cross on a field of red. In some dogs, the forechest marking is more like a shirtfront than the emblematic cross and is perfectly acceptable.

Even this puppy's coat shows the wonderfully distinctive markings of the Bernese Mountain Dog.

Puppies are born with a rather washed out rust color resembling café au lait. It gradually darkens and richens in color as the puppies get older. Even by eight weeks, the coloration is still more tan than rust. Often the eyespots and facial markings are somewhat deeper in tone at that age. The most reliable indicator of future depth of color is that of the parents. The brown markings in adult Bernese Mountain Dogs do vary, with deep russet being preferred to faded rust. Puppies often have a small patch of white on the back of the neck. This usually disappears or diminishes when the puppy changes coat. A helpful tool in assessing the likelihood of the spot remaining is to check the color of the skin below the white hairs. If it is pink, there will be white hair in that area. If the color of the skin is bluish gray, the white spot will most likely disappear with the growth of new coat.

GAIT

The natural working gait of the Bernese Mountain Dog is a slow trot. However, in keeping with his use in draft and droving work, he is capable of speed and agility. There is good reach in front. Powerful drive from the rear is transmitted through a level back. There is no wasted action. Front and rear legs on each side follow through in the same plane. At increased speed, legs tend to converge toward the center line.

Correct movement should reflect strength and convey the immediate impression of balance and effortless action along with the stamina needed for pulling a cart or driving livestock.

TEMPERAMENT

*The **temperament** is self-confident, alert and good-natured, never sharp or shy. The Bernese Mountain Dog should stand steady, though may remain aloof to the attentions of strangers*

The typical Bernese Mountain Dog has a pleasant, assured manner with a forthright attitude usually characterized by a wagging tail. He should show no signs of being aggressive or shy. An aloof dog that stands steady is not faulted. It is tremendously important to differentiate between shyness and aloofness since they are

LIMITED REGISTRATION

The AKC provides breeders with two options in designating the registration status of each puppy. These designations are full or limited registration. Limited registration means that puppies produced by that dog cannot be registered with the AKC and that the dog is ineligible to compete in conformation (breed competition) showing. He is eligible for all other AKC-licensed events, such as obedience or agility. Limited registration is designed to allow breeders to protect their breed and/or breeding program. Puppies identified as pets at the time of the transfer of ownership are usually sold on limited registration. This can be changed to full registration upon written request from the litter owner(s). The AKC requires a fee and a form to be completed by the litter owner(s) to redesignate registration status. If a change to full registration is being made to enable a litter to be eligible for AKC registration, that change must be made prior to breeding. For a litter to be eligible for registration with the AKC, both parents must be on full registration at the time of the breeding as well as when the litter is produced.

easily confused. Shyness, often detected by a dog's unwillingness to be touched by a stranger, even when encouraged by its handler, is undesirable. Aloofness, an acceptable response, is indifference with no outward display of liking or disliking attention from a stranger.

Bernese Mountain Dogs are happiest when surrounded by family and friends. They have a special affinity for children, responding to their attentions with remarkable sensitivity and an uncanny ability to modify their actions to accommodate behavioral differences in younger and older children. By nature, Bernese Mountain Dogs get along well with other animals. Easily

Both children and adults love the warm personalities of Berners.

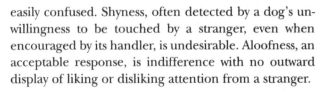

trained, their whole demeanor reveals an intense desire to please and to be a part of the home. It is not a breed to be relegated to a kennel or pen.

If a dog is raised with little contact with people other than family, aloofness with newcomers may result. For optimum enjoyment of a Bernese Mountain Dog, socialization and experiences away from home should accompany puppy training during the first year.

Faithful Friend and Perfect Partner

While the magnetic attraction to Bernese Mountain Dogs often begins with their stunning beauty, it is the natural disposition of the breed that captures the heart. All Bernese are pets, but some are given the specific designation of pet because of deviations from the standard. Such puppies are usually sold on limited registration with the AKC. Markings need not be perfect nor every ideal quality of the standard fulfilled to enjoy the greatest attribute of the Bernese Mountain Dog: total devotion as a friend and partner in making each day better and brighter.

chapter 2

The **Bernese Mountain Dog's Ancestry**

The actual origins of the Bernese Mountain Dog are shrouded in mystery. Archaeological digs in the areas inhabited by the Swiss "lake dweller people" reveal that there were dogs present as far back as 2000 to 3000 BC during the Neolithic period. To the puzzle of the breed's ancestry can be added the probable influence of large Mastiff-type dogs that came across the Alps with Roman legions more than two thousand years ago. It was their function to drive the livestock needed for provisioning

the army and to serve as camp protectors against marauding wolves and bears. The trade routes to the Roman provinces and the influence on the present-day language along those routes support the infusion of dog types from the Italian peninsula.

Four Alpine Breeds

Over time, four distinct Alpine working dogs developed in different areas of Switzerland where they are known as *Sennenhunde* (Alpine Herdsman's Dogs). Their heritage is so indigenous to Switzerland that they are considered the "national dogs." All have the distinctive tri-color markings of black, rust, and white. They are, from the smallest to the largest: the Entlebucher Sennenhunde, a short-coated, small dog, 15.5 inches to 17.5 inches, with a natural stump tail; the Appenzeller Sennenhunde, a ring-tailed, short coated, medium size dog 19.5 inches to 21.5 inches; the Berner Sennenhunde (Bernese Mountain Dog), a long coated, large dog, 23 inches to 27.5 inches with a long tail; and the Grosse Schweitzer Sennenhunde, translated as Great Swiss Mountain Dog and known in the United States as the Greater Swiss Mountain Dog, a short coated, large dog, 23.5 inches to 28.5 inches, with a long tail. It is believed that the Greater Swiss Mountain Dog is the oldest of the four breeds and was significant in the development of the Saint Bernard and the Rottweiler. Of the four Sennenhunde, only the Bernese has a long coat. AKC recognition was granted to the Bernese Mountain Dog in 1937 and to the Greater Swiss Mountain Dog in 1995.

The Swiss Farmer's Dog

A single thread of continuity influenced the development of the farmer's dogs: utility. There were no kennel clubs, breeding programs, or fanciers to accomplish this goal. Utility remained a hallmark of the breed due to the keen eye of the farmer who knew well how to improve his stock to get what he needed. A good, useful farm dog was no exception to the rule.

Just when the Bernese Mountain Dog emerged as an identifiable breed is not known. As a farmer's dog, the breed was not a subject of interest that might be documented in contemporary writings and art as happened with the hunting dogs and fashionable pets of the upper classes. However, a painting does exist—done in 1651 by Paulus Potter, a Dutch artist whose subjects were almost exclusively animals in landscape. It includes a dog that is clearly a Bernese Mountain Dog. With trade being extensive throughout Europe and especially along the Rhine Valley, the probability of Swiss farmers bringing herds of cattle with the help of their dogs to market in the Netherlands would explain the presence of this dog in a Dutch painting.

WHAT WERE THEY CALLED?

Unnamed as a breed, these dogs were designated by the work they did or by their markings, dependent upon locale. They were the cheese maker's dogs, butcher's dogs, and basket weaver's dogs in some areas while in others they were "yellow cheeks" or "four eyes" for their combined eyes and eyespots.

Your new Berner friend descended from farm dogs in Switzerland.

THE WORK THEY DID

On Swiss farms, the dog was not only a companion, but also another worker. The tasks demanded of him were varied and numerous, dependent upon need and the time of year. A day could easily include driving a small herd of cows to pasture or market; pulling a cart laden with milk cans, wheels of cheese, or whatever was needed; and, making the rounds with the master or mistress.

In summer, cattle, wearing their dulcet toned bells, would be driven to higher pasture for grazing to allow the valley fields to grow hay for the winter months ahead. Milking chores, now a long distance from the farm, still continued. A pair of the big, trustworthy, black, rust and white dogs would be harnessed to a cart loaded with freshly washed milk cans to make the rugged trip upland in the company of the farmer. He would milk the cows, fill the hefty cans, and return to the farm. The heavily laden cart required cautious braking by the farmer and his dogs as they maneuvered the often steep, downhill descent.

Because farmers originally bred Bernese Mountain Dogs to help them with chores, Berners still enjoy pulling carts today.

Little wonder that the descendants of those working dogs eagerly participate in present-day carting exhibitions and draft tests. Nothing is happier than a full-grown Bernese Mountain Dog pulling a sled load of youngsters on a wintery day.

Almost Lost to Posterity

With the popularity of the Saint Bernard escalating in the second half of the 19th century and the arrival in Switzerland of various foreign breeds, the future of the farmer's dogs seemed, after centuries of service, destined to oblivion. The old had given way to the new. It would not be until the late 19th century that the farmer's dogs gained attention as part of a spiraling interest in the sport of dogs. "Yellow cheeks" were already being reminisced about as faithful dogs of bygone days. Fortunately, two men in particular would be instrumental in restoring these dogs to their former place of importance as valuable working dogs and to bring about recognition of them as a distinct Swiss breed. The problem was where to find the few dogs that remained.

TWO WHO SAVED THE BREED

One of these men, Franz Schertenlieb, inspired by his father's recollections of wonderful dogs that were once commonplace, initiated a search in 1892 to find them. In some areas in the Canton of Bern, people spoke of a type of dog they called *Durrbachler*. This led Schertenlieb to a mountainous region south of the capital city of Bern in the district of Durrbach. There, dogs fitting his father's description could be seen pulling carts laden with milk cans, wheels of cheese, or baskets along twisting dirt roads or moving with a herd of livestock. With the acquisition of a Durrbachler, the "yellow cheeks" of old, Schertenlieb was able to spark a surge of interest among Swiss dog fanciers. During this critical period in bringing attention to this almost forgotten breed, the inn at Durrbach, which still stands, became a gathering place for the growing number of the breed's enthusiasts. The perseverance generated by these gentlemen culminated in 1905 with four Durrbachlers being registered by the Swiss Kennel Club. The numbers later increased with the addition of specimens deemed worthy of registry.

The second of the two men most responsible for the preservation and promotion of the breed, identified as Durrbachler, was Albert Heim, Professor of Geology at the University of Zurich. This highly respected dog fancier brought objectivity, skilled research techniques and, most of all, a unifying sense of direction in preserving the best qualities of the Alpine breeds. His contributions were so significant that he is often regarded as the father of the Bernese Mountain Dog.

How the Breed Got Its Name

At the suggestion of Professor Heim in 1908, the name Durrbachler was dropped in favor of *Berner Sennenhund* that he felt more correctly reflected the breed's origin in the Canton of Bern rather than just the small district of Durrbach. An Alpine herdsman is known as a Senn, so the name actually means Bernese Alpine Herdsman's Dog.

In English speaking countries, the breed is known as the Bernese Mountain Dog. Berner would be translated as Bernese with Mountain Dog referring to the breed being one of the four Swiss mountain dogs. A fascinating article providing the history and extolling the virtues of Bernese appeared in the *AKC Gazette*, June 1, 1935, by Mrs. L. Egg-Leach, an English sportswoman residing in Switzerland. The name she used throughout the article was Bernese until the last paragraph when she wrote, "I hope the time will come when the Bernese mountain dogs may be called 'a coming breed' on the other side of the Atlantic."

American owners today have brought the adorable working Berner into their homes.

Arrival in America

It would also be childhood memories that inspired the importation of Bernese Mountatin Dogs to America. Glen L. Shadow of Louisiana eagerly read and reread Mrs. Egg-Leach's article, "The Bernese Is a Loyal Dog of the Swiss Alps." These were the same dogs that he had so admired as a child in the pictures in his beginning reader showing dogs pulling milk carts. Years later, as a young man in France during 1918-19, he saw the dogs in real life. Sadly, his financial circumstances were such that he was unable to indulge his great desire to purchase one.

Almost 20 years later, Mr. Shadow was finally in a position to pursue his interest. Enthusiastically, he began a lengthy exchange of correspondence with Mrs. Egg-Leach to enlist her efforts in making his childhood dream a reality. Her tireless search on his behalf finally resulted in her being able to purchase an outstanding pair of Bernese for Mr. Shadow. Arriving in America on November 10, 1936 on the *S.S. Normandie* was the best female in all Europe, Fridy v. Haslenbach. She was accompanied by Quell v. Tiergarten who was to be her mate. These were the first Bernese Mountain Dogs to be registered by the AKC, with official recognition of the breed as a member of the Working Group being granted on April 13, 1937.

Fridy was such a prototype for the future that her photograph was matched with a look-alike champion female in 1987, fifty years later! This is indeed testimony to the breed's purity.

While the milestone of acceptance by the AKC is forever to the credit of Glen Shadow, not a dog today exists that can trace its ancestry to this famous first pair. Although they did produce litters, a continuous line was never established from any of Mr. Shadow's dogs despite efforts that weathered the war years and extended as far as 1961.

Some Who Share the Companionship of a Berner

The handsome looks and good-natured temperament of the Bernese Mountain Dog draws owners from all walks of life. Robert Redford, distinguished actor and environmentalist, was attracted to the breed in the 1970's, even becoming involved with breeding them at his ranch in Sundance, Utah, under the kennel name of Double R. His fondness for the breed continues to the present with just one Berner, Duchess, a lovely female, who lives with Mr. Redford at the ranch.

FAMOUS BERNESE MOUNTAIN DOG OWNERS
David Caradine
Robert Duncan
Nick Faldo
Charles Gibson
Mark Harmon
Goldie Hawn
François Mitterand
Robert Redford
William Saffire

William Safire, political columnist for the *New York Times*, has owned Berners for many years. When a particularly favorite dog passed away, he extolled the virtues of his faithful Bernese in his column.

The artistic beauty of Berners has so captured the imagination of Robert Duncan that he has created a series of paintings portraying his own dogs at play with his children. Another artist, the late Joyce Miller, created an entire series of children's items in the 1970's for Sears' catalog featuring "Grandma and Grandpa" and their Bernese, "Joe Dog" who had one blue and one brown eye. He was modeled after her own Joe Dog with the same eye color. Joyce's real life Berner always accompanied her on promotions for her unique work that included a patchwork quilt of "Grandma, Grandpa, and Joe Dog" and a stuffed, toy Berner with the trademark blue and brown eyes. These collectibles can sometimes be spotted at yard sales.

The celebrated culinary expert, Julia Child, has mentioned the breed as being a welcome houseguest during the holidays when friends have joined her with their big, beautiful Berner, Abigail. Just imagine the gourmet table scraps!

While it is exciting to share the limelight of owning a Bernese Mountain Dog with the famous, the real joy of ownership is in having a dog that will always be your number one fan. Television host, Charles Gibson, commented about his Berner, "He's there at the front door when I come home."

It's easy to see why Berners are big favorites, especially with celebrities!

24

chapter 3

The **World**

According to

the **Bernese**

Mountain Dog

The single, most important component of a Bernese Mountain Dog's world is family, whether one person or a brimming houseful. For this reason, he is not suited to live his life in a kennel or to being kept apart from the everyday functions of being a part of the home. A Bernese Mountain Dog must be considered a member of the family. He can adapt to almost any sit-

uation or schedule as long as several hours of each day include interaction with him. If a Berner could speak, he would say, "Let me be with you. Let me walk by your side, share your joys and sorrows, and work with you as we train together to develop my intelligence so I may better serve you. In return, I will give you a lifetime of loyalty."

25

Lifetime Commitment

The ownership of a Bernese Mountain Dog should not be undertaken lightly. Conscientious breeders will carefully interview potential owners with significant emphasis on assuring the welfare of the puppy for the entirety of his life. The Bernese Mountain Dog's natural loyalty and devotion to family demand lifetime commitment. A puppy joins its new family with 100% trust and dependence.

While some wonderful successes in placing older Berners in second homes have been accomplished, this has only been done through the diligence of owners, breeders, and rescue groups who are determined to fulfill their responsibility to each dog. There are cases that dramatically demand acceptance of lifetime commitment.

Understanding a Berner

Your new Berner longs to spend some quality time with you.

Capitalizing on a Berner's desire to please eases his training. From the beginning, consistency, patience and praise are essential. He may not always understand what is expected, but a Berner is extremely impressionable, particularly when it comes to negative experiences. For this reason, your Berner's reactions of uncertainty or fearfulness should be treated in an up-beat manner rather than encouraging the behavior with petting and soothing entonements of, "That's okay, you'll be all right." Instead, keep your voice and body-language enthusiastic. Situations that are positive and result in desired behavior should be reinforced with praise.

A Berner needs to be introduced to the world beyond his home at an early age. Socialization in a wide variety of settings and experiences develops self-assurance. If socialization is neglected in the first six to eight months of a Berner's life, he may find it difficult to adjust to new situations despite being completely out-going at home. Success builds confidence, failure undermines it.

BERNER SIGN LANGUAGE

A Berner's interaction with his humans reveals some typical mannerisms. Reminiscent of bears, the front paws are used for communication. From early puppyhood, a single paw may be raised to express hello; I don't want to; or, how about petting me? It's the Berner peace symbol with other dogs. With increased height, requests for continued petting include elbow bumping with the nose, a risky experience if you are holding a hot cup of coffee! Affectionately, Berners will lean into a person, sit on a foot, or even try climbing onto an open lap.

Caesar, a 95-pound male that had never

> ### THE BERNER BEAR
>
> With puppies like teddy bears and the breed's playful, bear-like mannerisms, it is only natural to associate Bernese Mountain Dogs with bears. The Swiss long-ago recognized the resemblance by the use of the term, "barri" or "little bear," to describe Berners that were mostly black and rust.

out-grown his desire to be a lap dog, learned to await his owner's invitation with, "It's baby-boy time." He would then ensconce the front half of his body on his owner's lap for treasured minutes of petting.

Socializing your puppy ensures that training will go smoothly as she grows.

The Berner's success as a housedog is partly attributable to his amazing comprehension of giving as much or as little of himself as his family seeks. Most Bernese are laid-back and easy to settle down. A Berner can have his moments though of playful mischief, stubbornness, and comedy. The happy Berner has a special way of pulling the corners of his mouth up in what surely must be a canine smile.

Doing Things Together

Versatility of ability in the Bernese Mountain Dog makes him an ideal candidate for a wide range of activities. Basic obedience is an excellent starting point because it forms a foundation for pursuit of everything else. In all instances, the dog's maturity and physical fitness in relation to the type of activity should be taken into consideration. For example, young dogs have a high energy level; however, their growing bodies would not be developed enough for pounding the pavement with a jogger. More slowly-paced hiking and backpacking would be better for younger dogs. There are even canine backpacks for the dog to carry his own provisions, with lighter loads, of course, for younger dogs.

Bicycles and Berners make a great combination.

The Berner's scope of companionship is determined by the extent of how much he is allowed to participate. From his standpoint, the more the better. Though not water dogs by nature, some enjoy swimming. Berners can be found in some unexpected places: Maggie goes sailing regularly with her family; Oakley accompanies his mistress daily in her work as a gardener at exclusive properties; and Tell serves as the mascot for his young master's soccer team.

Berners are wonderful traveling companions, delighting in trips to the grocery store or to pick up the kids from school. It doesn't take long for the rattle of keys to become the signal to go "bye-bye." The dog's safety while riding should be insured by using a pet seat-belt restraint or by crating the dog. Do remember that in the summer a vehicle can become a lethal oven in a very few minutes even with partially open windows.

The satisfaction and sense of accomplishment gained from working a Berner in such activities as obedience, carting, agility, tracking, or herding can be truly fulfilling to dog and owner. The Bernese Mountain Dog Club of America (BMDCA), in its dedication to the preservation of the working characteristics of Bernese Mountain Dogs, encourages such participation by both show and pet Berners through a variety of incentives to recognize achievements. Membership is required for eligibility.

For the Love of a Child

Bernese Mountain Dogs are unbelievably attuned to children. They are remarkably sensitive to adjusting their tolerance levels to the age and capability of the child. This innate characteristic is so strong that even older Bernese, unused to the daily presence of children, are able to adjust to life with "little people." Under all circumstances, supervision and careful monitoring are mandatory for the safeguarding of children and pets. As family pets, day care mascots, and therapy dogs, Bernese distinguish themselves with attentiveness and just the right degree of affection.

Melody was just such a Berner. As a retired champion, she joined, at the age of 5, a young couple familiar with the breed. Two years later, the anticipated arrival of the couple's first child prompted great misgivings by

Bernese Mounain Dogs are exceptionally devoted to children.

friends and well-wishers about the dog's ability to accept a newborn. Fortunately, their unsolicited advice to get rid of Melody was ignored. Suddenly, the expectant parents were thrust into great difficulties with the pregnancy. Long-term, premature labor contractions, delayed sufficiently by drugs to prevent delivery, resulted in the birth of a little girl with only one leg. When the little girl, Nova, came home, she was warmly greeted by her long-haired nanny, Melody. The attentive dog, now seven, lovingly embarked upon the fulfillment of her life's mission. Nova's first attempts to stand were with the help of Melody, as were her steps with the first of many prostheses for the missing leg. As baby hands clung to the long fur of Melody's neck or a tearful head buried itself there, no stranger was permitted between the child and dog.

CHARACTERISTICS OF A BERNESE MOUNTAIN DOG

intelligent

self-confident

alert

good-natured

loyal

devoted to family

needs human companionship

Keeping the Berner Cool

While there is nothing quite as happy as a Bernese Mountain Dog in the snow, the breed functions very well in any climate if properly managed. The greatest concern is excessive heat. That is readily solved with air conditioning and outdoor periods safeguarded with access to plenty of natural shade. A Berner will take advantage of the smallest scrap of shade to get a reprieve from a blistering sun. Cool, fresh water should be available at all times, inside and outside. The long, black coat of the Bernese Mountain Dog makes him particularly vulnerable to rapid heat build-up when in the sun. During hot weather, it is essential to avoid

This smart Berner knows to head for a shade tree in hot weather.

walking or exercising a Berner in full sun for any length of time. Absorption of the sun's rays quickly turns his black coat into a heat blanket with no way to toss it off.

Unlike human beings, dogs can only perspire by panting and through the pads of their feet. It is not unusual to see a Berner select the coolest surface available and lie belly down with both hind legs stretched out behind. If left outside for any length of time when it is uncomfortably warm, a Berner will find as cool and damp a spot as possible and will promptly begin digging a hole in which to stay cool. With daily improvements and no interference, the hole may eventually be fashioned into a cavern big enough for the entire dog.

*His gorgeous
coat is part of
this Berner's
appeal, but keep
shedding season
in mind!*

That Beautiful Coat Does Shed

Shedding occurs most typically in the spring with the advent of warm weather. Sometimes dogs shed near their birthday. That cycle is associated with the process of shedding the first adult coat at about 1 year of age. The good thing is that Bernese normally do not shed year round. Once the coat starts to drop, the process can be hastened with a bath followed by heavy-duty brushing and combing. The latter should continue daily until the brush fails to be filled with hair. In a lazy, untidy household, neglecting the shed of a full-coated Bernese invites considerable discomfort to the dog, possibly requiring the services of a veterinarian to treat related skin problems (see Chapter 7, "Hotspots"), not to mention joking accusations that the cook seasons with Berner hair. Shaving a Bernese is not a solution to shedding because the outer coat acts as insulation and protection against flies.

31

What About Exercise?

With the Bernese, there is no perfect formula for what is needed when it comes to exercise. In relation to their size compared with other breeds, Berners are moderate in their needs for exercise and energy release. The perfect outlet for Berners is a fenced yard that is accessed directly from the house. In this safe environment, a Berner can romp, play, and train with his family. Along with yard play, neighborhood walks for socializing and exercise are greatly enjoyed as time together.

Running in the yard is a great outlet for this exuberant puppy's energy level.

If relying more on leash walking for exercise and energy release, a 30 to 40 minute walk twice daily in addition to outings for the dog to relieve himself should be adequate. In all instances, individual needs must be addressed as regards age and energy level.

Since they are so lovable, it's easy to want to have two Berner puppies at once. It's a better idea to wait awhile until the first puppy bonds to you and your family before adding another bundle of fur to the family.

Berners Enjoy the Company of Other Pets

The breed's heritage as a farm dog makes it highly receptive to being around other animals, both large and small. The companionship of a cat or another dog would be well received with proper introductions, whether bringing the Berner into a household with pets or if adding other pets later (see Chapter 4, "Introduction to Other Pets").

Definitely avoid the temptation to get two puppies at the same time, even if it is a different breed. The puppies will bond with each other rather than forming the strong relationship between dog and owner that can only be established without the distraction of another puppy in the critical, first few months with the family. Dividing time and training between two puppies is very challenging and hardly conducive to gaining maximum pleasure from either one.

Before bringing another puppy into the household, wait until the first one is *at least* 8 to 10 months old and has been spayed or neutered. By that time, your first dog's basic training and individual personality have been established. Assuming that the dogs are neutered or spayed, the most successful combinations, sex-wise, are male and female or two females. The potential of even neutered males to fight with one another at some point in time is too great a probability to take the risk. Most families who get a Berner decide that more than one is fun, a decision that gets paws up approval.

Life Expectancy

The companionship of a Bernese Mountain Dog is truly a joy. Unfortunately, the average life span is just 8 to 10 years, sometimes less. There are those that make it to the wonderful age of 12 or 13, but not nearly enough do. Cancer has

---

A DOG'S SENSES

Sight: With their eyes located farther apart than ours, dogs can detect movement at a greater distance than we can, but they can't see as well up close. They can also see better in less light, but can't distinguish many colors.

Sound: Dogs can hear about four times better than we can, and they can hear high-pitched sounds especially well. Their ancestors, the wolves, howled to let other wolves know where they were; our dogs do the same, but they have a wider range of vocalizations, including barks, whimpers, moans and whines.

Smell: A dog's nose is his greatest sensory organ. His sense of smell is so great he can follow a trail that's weeks old, detect odors diluted to one-millionth the concentration we'd need to notice them and even sniff out a person under water!

Taste: Dogs have fewer taste buds than we do, so they're likelier to try anything—and usually do, which is why it's especially important for their owners to monitor their food intake. Dogs are omnivores, which means they eat meat as well as vegetable matter like grasses and weeds.

Touch: Dogs are social animals and love to be petted, groomed and played with.

been identified as the major cause of death in Bernese Mountain Dogs and is becoming a significant cause for concern in other breeds as well (see Chapter 7, "Cancer"). Since 1989, the BMDCA has maintained a high profile in pursuing cancer research in Bernese Mountain Dogs. Additionally, it has taken a proactive approach to all health issues, including cancer, through *The Berner-Garde Foundation* that is dedicated to the understanding and reduction of genetic disease in Bernese Mountain Dogs. The BMDCA has an on-going database with information from as far back as 1974. Selective breeding for longevity and controlling the diet are two methods being employed by many breeders to address this health problem. For those who find the breed's characteristics a match to their life style, the rewards of owning a Bernese Mountain Dog more than counterbalance the risk of a shorter lifespan. Living with a Berner can truly be quality time.

Your Berner will be a loyal companion throughout his life.

More Information on the Bernese Mountain Dog

NATIONAL BREED CLUB

Bernese Mountain Dog Club of America
2121 S. Reserve Street # 370
Missoula, MT 59801
SASE Requested
E-Mail: BMDCA@ PHONL.COM

The national club can provide a general information brochure on the breed, guidelines to selecting a quality Bernese Mountain Dog from a reputable breeder, and a list of contact persons for each of the breed's regional clubs. Inquire about membership.

BOOKS

Cochrane, Diana. *The Bernese Mountain Dog.* Great Britain: Westgrove House, 1987.

Russ, Diane & Shirle Rogers. *The Beautiful Bernese Mountain Dog.* Colorado: Alpine Publications, 1993.

Simonds, Jude. *The Complete Bernese Mountain Dog.* New York: Howell Book House, 1990.

Smith, Sharon Chestnutt. *The New Bernese Mountain Dog.* New York: Howell Book House, 1994.

MAGAZINES

BMDCA. *The Alpenhorn.* 1338 W. Park Street, Arlington Heights, IL 60005.

Living
with a

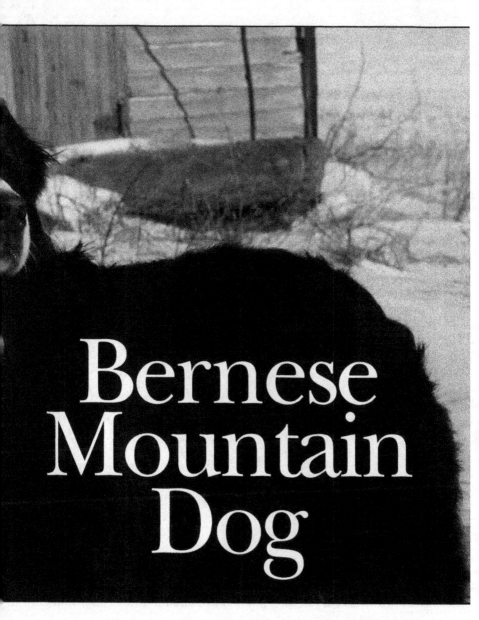

part two

Bernese Mountain Dog

chapter 4

Bringing
Your Bernese
Mountain Dog
Home

Deciding whether to actually bring home a Berner puppy requires more than just determining if this breed is right for you. It demands careful self-assessment. Are you and everyone in the family ready for the *commitment?* Do you really have the *time* and *place* for a puppy and the adult she will become? Finding the answers to these questions and others will happen through research, and most importantly, through talking and visiting with reliable, experienced breeders who should give an overwhelming impression of concern for proper placement of a Bernese puppy. A Bernese Mountain Dog's inherent desire to please and to be a part of the family dictates the need for a home that will treat her as a member of the household.

Expect to be asked a lot of questions about your plans for the dog's future and your ability to provide adequate care. Honest answers will help the breeder give you the best possible guidance. You, in turn, should ask about the parents' temperament and health clearances regarding hips, elbows, and eyes (see Chapter 7, "Specific Health Concerns for the Bernese Mountain Dog"). In choosing a puppy, let your head, not your heart rule. While your initial attraction to Bernese Mountain Dogs may have been motivated by their appearance, it is the temperament of the breed that makes it a superlative companion (see Chapter 1, "Temperament"). In looking at a litter of Berners, it is easy to be overly influenced by markings. Assessment of a Berner puppy must be a blend of how she looks and her individual personality. Be prepared to wait for the right puppy.

PUPPY ESSENTIALS

Your new puppy will need the following items:

food bowl

water bowl

collar

leash

ID tag

bed

crate

toys

grooming supplies

The long-awaited day to bring home your Bernese Mountain Dog puppy should be preceded by considerable preparation in anticipation of her arrival. The earliest that you can expect to bring her home would be at 7 to 9 weeks of age. This is her debut as a new member of the family and making it a successful introduction to your world requires purchasing basic equipment, puppy-proofing the home, and planning a schedule in advance of the big day.

In the event that your new arrival is an older puppy or an adult Bernese Mountain Dog, many of the preparations will be the same. The puppy's adjustment to your home will be greatly facilitated by learning as much as you can about her previous home. The most important thing, regardless of age, is patience and lots of love.

Basic Equipment for Now and Later

A CRATE

A good quality, collapsible crate that is large enough to accommodate the puppy when it is an adult is a priority purchase. It should be of heavy gauge wire with secure, easy-to-operate latches and a removable bottom tray. While enclosed airline type crates made of heavy-duty plastic can be suitable for temporary crating during the first few days, the wire crate is recommended for crate training because it lets the puppy see what is going on and is light and airy. A crate that is approximately 26" wide × 42" long × 30" high is large enough for most adult Berners.

This adult Berner tries his crate on for size. You may want to purchase a large crate even when your puppy is still small. As you can see, he will grow into it!

BABY GATES

The wide range of size and portability of baby gates makes them ideal for confining the puppy to designated areas. If put in use early on, most adult Berners will honor such barriers. Gates for standard door sizes or wide openings between living areas are available with swing-style access for easy passage. Restricted areas can now be managed easily and attractively.

Collars.

Start out with inexpensive leashes and collars because the growing Berner will quickly outgrow collars—and leashes are readily chewed. The first collar for an eight or nine week old Berner should be a size 14-inch narrow, nylon puppy collar that adjusts to any length by finding its own hole. After that, the most satisfactory are the adjustable, quick snap buckle collars for I.D. tag's and general wear, if required.

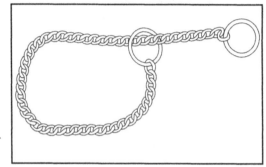

The standard collar used for formal training is the chain choke collar, although some prefer a nylon choke. *There is a right way and a wrong way to put on a choke collar. Do not use a choke collar until you know how to put it on your Berner.* Worn correctly, it has a choke/release effect; incorrectly, it has a choke/no release effect. *Never leave a choke collar on an unattended dog. An alternative to the choke collar to achieve control is the relatively new, halter type head collar.*

This is the proper way to place a choke collar on your dog.

This Berner puppy seems to be used to her leash already.

Leashes

The first leash should be 4-foot nylon leash, most likely the same material as the collar. While vulnerable to chewing, it is ideal for getting your puppy acquainted with walking on a lead. After your puppy has accepted walking on a leash, move up to a 6-foot long × $1/2$-inch wide inexpensive web training leash. Once it is established that a leash is for walking, not chewing, invest in a quality latigo or twisted latigo leash. This soft leather leash is handsome and easy on the hands.

Your Berner should not be allowed to carry her leash in her mouth when walking on lead. While very cute, it indicates, "I'm in control." Maintenance of your authority is important. Application of a chew deterrent spray will eliminate the temptation to carry the leash.

Wonderfully fun, retractable leads permit a sense of real freedom while maintaining control. These are terrific for parks, beaches, anywhere that it is safe for your Berner to range. Do keep in mind that the farther away she gets, the more power she has to pull. The retractable variety of leash is not satisfactory for areas demanding close control, such as the veterinary office or in-town walking.

IDENTIFICATION TAGS TO SAFEGUARD YOUR BERNER

Making sure your Berner has a legible ID tag is part of being a responsible owner.

As soon as possible, get an identification tag for your Berner's collar. It may include the dog's name and your address and phone number with the area code. Some prefer giving only the phone number. Periodically, check the tag to be sure that it is clearly readable.

There are two additional options for identification of your Berner. Permanent identification with a microchip is especially valuable since it is a positive, lifelong identification of the dog and is not dependent on a collar. *HomeAgain* is a microchip identification system that can be implanted in between the shoulder blades by your veterinarian. Enrollment with the AKC Companion Animal Recovery Program provides 24-hour phone service to reunite pet and owner. Most animal shelters and veterinarians have scanners that can read the ID code to start the process.

Tattooing is another form of ID. The drawbacks are that it can fade and have no contact source. If used, the owner's Social Security number is often suggested. The major advantage is that no scanner is needed. Some elect to have all three forms of ID for maximum safety in the event of the unexpected.

Bowls for Food and Water

Crock-style plastic dishes are non-breakable and don't make an unpleasant noise when moved across the floor by a hungry pup cleaning the bowl. Since some Berners like to play in the water dish, a non-tip water bowl is the best choice. This can be a crock-style stoneware or flared-side, stainless-steel bowl.

Clean-up Tools

Pet waste should be scooped up frequently with one of the many products designed for this purpose. Begin this process as soon as your Berner arrives. When walking off the property or traveling, always pick up feces no matter what other, less responsible owners may do. This unpleasant task has been greatly improved with special bags for cleanup.

Toys, Toys, Toys— The More the Better

A few toys of varying types should be available for the Berner puppy's arrival. A soft fleece toy is especially important. After all, she won't have her brothers and sisters to nuzzle, so that cuddly fleece squeak toy will be a big hit. She will decide on favorites. As she gets older, her interests will expand, but most likely there will be one, special toy. However, frequent, new additions are always welcome. Make a big event over newly presented playthings. With all the excitement, she will need to go out as soon as she stops playing. At gift giving time, be sure to include her on the list. She'll be as excited over her wrapped toy as anyone else. Help her unwrap her treasure, taking care to prevent her from eating the paper. Toys may seem like meaningless extravagances, but they definitely stimulate mental development while providing entertainment.

Carefully inspect toys for safety, even those specifically offered for dogs may have some feature that could be hazardous. Latex toys are surprisingly durable. Plush toys are always treasured, but be sure to supervise your puppy if the toy has a squeaker. The puppy may be able to tear the fabric, retrieve the squeaker and try to swallow it. Hard rubber, Kong-type toys are great, as are those that can be played with by you and the puppy, such as balls.

Children in the family need to be cautioned that their toys can easily be interpreted by the puppy as being for her. Care should be

Toys help baby Berners develop motor skills they will use throughout their lives.

taken to recognize that safe toys for children may be dangerous for the puppy. A special box for the puppy's toys can help remind children to safely store their own toys when finished playing with them.

Chew toys are particularly helpful during the teething period. In fact, Berners never outgrow the enjoyment of chewing a bone. Rawhide chews can be very dangerous when they are too small, start to segment, or knobby ends come off. These are highly vulnerable to swallowing, which can result in choking or intestinal blockage. If used, rawhides should be given with supervision and awareness that once they start to unravel they should be discarded. Much preferred are flavored or natural bones that can be purchased at pet centers. For outdoor enjoyment, a fresh, uncooked beef marrow bone can't be surpassed. Choose a long, bone that can't be swallowed easily.

Early on, teach your Berner to relinquish a toy or bone, using the term, "Give." Reward the response with praise and the return of the object, a substitute, or a treat. This is an invaluable safeguard in protecting a child attempting to take something from the dog's mouth and in preparing your Berner to release something that may be harmful.

Besides being an outlet for enjoyment, play and chewing, the right toys also make excellent training aids. See Chapter 8, "Basic Training," for advice on how to use chew toys to prevent mischief and common behavior problems simply and easily.

BERNER BED

Most Berners love to stretch out on a cool surface, even in winter. Once a preferred spot becomes obvious, a rug may be placed there. To see if investing in a bed is worthwhile, the crate mat can be put in that location. Some Berners do enjoy a bed while others will opt for anyplace near you. All would be delighted to share your bed!

From an early age, Kodi persuaded her master and mistress to allow her on the bed. She would start the night there, then move to the floor to sleep until early morning when she would return to snuggle with her human companions as they awakened. Remember, once started it isn't easy to enforce "no" later. A Berner, wet from her final evening walk on a cold, rainy night is hardly welcome to share anyone's bed!

It's naptime on the crate mat for this puppy.

Puppyproofing Preparation

There is nothing like a puppy or a toddler to remind adults to keep things out of reach. Berners are quick to become civilized household members, however some basic puppyproofing needs to be done to prevent upsets, heartbreaks or tragedies.

FOR THE HOME

While the ultimate goal is for your Berner to have access to the entire house, that must be postponed until she has become reliably housebroken (see Chapter 8, "Basic Training"). Begin by limiting her to an area that can be monitored and cleaned easily in the event of an accident. Carefully inspect any area where the puppy may venture for potential hazards or possible unwanted destruction. Electrical cords are the most obvious, but anything that is within a curious Berner's reach while standing on her hind legs should be evaluated for vulnerability. Household, automotive, and garden chemicals in the home and garage should be safely stored. Antifreeze leaked onto a garage floor is sweet tasting and highly poisonous Chapter 7, "Accidental Poisoning").

HOUSEHOLD DANGERS

Curious puppies and inquisitive dogs get into trouble not because they are bad, but simply because they want to investigate the world around them. It's our job to protect our dogs from harmful substances, like the following:

In the Garage

antifreeze

garden supplies, like snail and slug bait, pesticides, fertilizers and mouse and rat poisons

In the House

cleaners, especially pine oil

perfumes, colognes and after-shaves

medications and vitamins

office and craft supplies

electrical cords

chicken and turkey bones

chocolate and onions

some house and garden plants, like ivy, oleander and poinsettia

---

THE YARD

Check fence lines for gaps large enough for a puppy to get through. Secure these and any other areas that might be enticing, such as the cool, den-like atmosphere beneath a deck or under a house or outbuilding. If there is a garden or some shrubbery that is to be off-limits, it should be protected and the puppy safeguarded from the poisonous shrubs, such as rhododendrons, azaleas, and yews. Toadstools can be poisonous, so they should be removed. Hoses and gardening equipment must be put away after use or they will be considered the latest toy. Periodically check the premises to maintain it as a safe environment for the growing Berner.

Selecting a Name

Just what to call a puppy can take hours of discussion and research. You may decide to wait until she comes home to see what fits her personality. It is very important to select a name that does not rhyme with a frequently used command or with a family member's name. These choices can create a great deal of confusion. For example, Neil rhymes with heel, the command for walking at one's side. Think carefully about whether the call name will conflict with words used in training or correction. Definitely avoid a name that would rhyme with "No." Names of one or two syllables work well.

The Ride Home

The ride home, whether from the breeder or the airport, should be as pleasant as possible. If at all fea-

"Gooooood dog!" This puppy comes running at the sound of her name.

sible, schedule the arrival home early in the day so the puppy will have time to settle in before bedtime. Bring along a collar and leash, a crate or large box and newspapers with which to line it, paper towels, a couple of plastic trash bags, an old bath towel, a bowl, water, and a toy or two for the puppy's entertainment. If the driver is traveling alone, the puppy should be secured in a crate. For maximum enjoyment by the proud family and the puppy, riding on a passenger's towel-covered lap is the best way to start.

The puppy should have on a very lightweight leash and collar for her safety. *Both collar and leash must be removed when crating or leaving the puppy unattended, even for a short time.* The crate, lined with newspaper and shredded newspaper, should be available to put the puppy in when she becomes too wiggly or unmanageable during the ride home. Playing the radio at low to medium levels may help calm the puppy and soothe the driver if the puppy cries. If the trip is fairly long or from the airport, the puppy will need an opportunity to relieve herself. Try to select a grassy area that is unlikely to have been visited by other dogs. Even though the puppy should have begun the series of vaccinations, she is still vulnerable to a variety of canine illnesses. No matter how much the puppy may be distracted by the newness of a collar and leash, do not let her loose. An unexpected noise or event can send the puppy scurrying into harm's way at a surprisingly uncatchable rate.

Establishing a Routine

The first few nights are usually the most difficult for the new arrival. To make the transition to her new home as smooth as possible, follow the schedule she is accustomed to as closely as is feasible. If changes are necessary, make them gradually. One likely exception will be the last time out before retiring. That will probably be much later than what had been the litter's bedtime. Locate your puppy's crate in a quite place for sleeping. Prepare it with a towel and/or shredded newspapers so that she has something to snuggle. A fleece toy is an appropriate bedtime toy. Most likely she will do some crying upon being put to bed. Lights out should become a signal that it is time to go to sleep. If you are certain that your puppy's basic needs have been filled, ignore her complaints. Later in the night, her cries may indicate a need to relieve herself. Some owners find crating the puppy in their bedroom hastens the bonding process and permits attentive reaction to housebreaking. Do expect to take the puppy out during the night. Even so, she may have soiled her crate despite her basic inclination to be clean. Be patient, she will learn as her time clock adjusts to your household schedule—and remember, a young puppy can only wait so long.

FORMAL NAMES

The name for AKC registration, which is the dog's formal name, may have some specific requirements made by the breeder. In most instances, the kennel name will be used as a prefix to be followed by a name that may or may not be the dog's call name. The breeder may also stipulate a naming scheme, such as alphabetical sequence for litter identification. That is a practice commonly used in Switzerland. Puppies from the breeder's first litter would carry as the first name after the kennel name an adjective or name starting with the letter "A," with those from the second being "B," etc.

The morning wake-up for your Berner will be at the time she has been accustomed to. Take her outside immediately, followed by feeding and outside again. Her day should be a healthy blend of play, getting acquainted with her surroundings, quiet time in her crate, and outside trips after each meal, upon awakening from a nap, and after playing. Meals should be offered at approximately the same time each day (see "Feeding the Berner Puppy," Chapter 5.

After the first two or three days, each day should include very brief, upbeat leash training experiences. Once the household manners that will be expected of your Berner puppy have been determined, everyone in the family must be consistent in helping the puppy learn them. Use of the same terms for desired behavior will make it much easier for her. If there are special expectations that you would like to establish, such as having her feet wiped off before entering the house or using a particular spot in the yard for elimination, this is the time to begin. Puppy behavior that will be obnoxious as an adult needs to be redirected. For example, jumping up to be petted, may be redirected by stooping down to the puppy's height while giving gentle encouragement to sit when greeting you and guests. Remember, what is cute as a puppy may not be cute as an adult. Enrollment in puppy kindergarten will provide you with techniques for training and her with socialization (see Chapter 8, "Basic Training").

Introduction to Other Pets

If there is already a cat or dog in the family, they should be secured in a part of the house that your Berner will not be exploring in her first introduction to her new home. This should be done *before* bringing the puppy inside. Give her plenty of time for looking around, getting a drink of water and even being fed. When she seems to be at ease, introductions can begin. Don't rush things. Your puppy will need time to absorb all that is happening. If waiting until the next day for the big meeting seems appropriate, then do so. Berner puppies are trusting, and the sight of another dog or a kitty that's her size will energize her enthusiasm to make friends. It is important to realize that your established pet's reaction may not be the same. Most of all, they should be made to feel special, too. Make sure they're included in getting new toys and treats.

MEETING THE RESIDENT DOG

When your Berner puppy is secure with her new surroundings, put your resident dog on a leash so that he can be controlled. If the puppy is especially effervescent, she should also be leashed. In conducting introductions, take into consideration how the resident dog has behaved with strange dogs in the past. This knowledge will be helpful in orchestrating a successful meeting. When the two meet, there will be plenty of sniffing. Talk encouragingly in positive tones of voice and give lots of petting to the older dog and the puppy. If all is going well, they can be permitted to walk around off leash. In the event that the resident dog objects to the new puppy, repeat the process of introductions several times during the day. It is important to conclude the meeting when things are going well. Supervision is absolutely necessary, in the weeks ahead no matter how well things are going.

A large dog can easily hurt a puppy in his enthusiasm for getting to know her. For this reason, supervision is absolutely necessary not only at this first meeting but in the weeks ahead. While your Berner puppy may be an eager partner in roughhousing, it can result in future orthopedic problems. Likewise, smaller dogs need protection from your new puppy. Additionally, a puppy can be very persistent in her attentions to her new friend, thereby stretching the tolerance level to a literal snapping point. A puppy should not be allowed to abuse the good nature of her new canine buddy.

MEETING THE RESIDENT CAT

Felines make their own rules. Let the cat take her time in meeting the Berner. Be sure that the cat has access to an escape route or something that she can jump on to be out of reach. This might be a good time to have the puppy on a leash. She will think that the kitty is a marvelous toy. Expect the cat to puff up and hiss even if used to a family dog. This establishes authority and creates the invisible line that a cat puts between herself and a dog. It may take several days or weeks before the cat fully accepts the puppy, but that is all part of a cat's charisma.

No matter how sweet your new puppy is, always be there to supervise when she meets the resident pet in your home.

Physical Precautions—Limit Stress on Growing Bones

As a large, rapid-growth breed with heavy bone structure, there are some ways to limit stress on your growing Berner besides keeping weight under control. When picking her up, do so all at one time by placing one hand under her rear and the other under her ribcage. This will distribute the weight between the front and rear. *Never pick up a puppy as you would a child by lifting it under the arms.* Unfortunately, not all owners are aware of the physical stress this places on the shoulders. While holding your Berner, keep her elbows in rather than letting one hook over your arm thereby placing stress on the shoulders. When putting the puppy down, have front and rear come down at the same time. Allowing a Berner to hop or leap from your

51

arms with the front paws landing first can be poten-
tially harmful to the shoulder assemblage. Assistance
should always be given the growing Berner when getting in and out of vehicles, particularly vans or those
vehicles high off the ground.

Children in the family and visiting youngsters must be
instructed as to what they can and can't do when they
play with the puppy. This will vary with the age of the
child and must be reviewed and updated as the puppy
grows. Picking up the puppy should be restricted to
adults. A Berner should not be climbed on or ridden,
no matter how big she may appear. She must not be
exercised by providing joy rides by pulling a youngster
on a skateboard or roller blades. Even though the
Berner may be an eager participant as she gallops at
the end of her leash with the rider gliding along
behind, this type of strain on the musculoskeletal system must not be permitted.

Particularly to be avoided is rough and tumble playtime with larger dogs or puppies. Although she may
enjoy it, lasting damage can be done that may not be
immediately observable. These precautions while she
is growing may seem to be a nuisance, but are well
worth the proverbial, ounce of prevention.

Got Questions?
They've Got Anwers!

The two most important resources to go to for help are
your Berner's breeder and your veterinarian. The
breeder should provide written vaccination/health
records as well as feeding and general care instructions. Conscientious, experienced breeders want to be
contacted in the event of questions or problems, and
some will encourage periodic updates for the lifetime
of the Berner. Calling the breeder for assistance should
be the first, not the last resort, and should be done
sooner rather than later. Concerns about diet, behavior, training, or health can usually be readily resolved
with input from your Berner's breeder. The benefit of
breed-specific experience cannot be over emphasized.

Next to you, a Berner's best friend is her veterinarian (see Chapter 7, "Selecting a Veterinarian"). That relationship will have begun on her initial visit, usually during the first 48 hours or as specified by the breeder in the puppy's transfer to your ownership. At that time, present a copy of the breeder's health records for the puppy. There is nothing quite as comforting as having a veterinarian and staff who are genuinely interested in helping you keep your Berner healthy.

Other owners of Bernese Mountain Dogs are great resources of information and fun for you and your puppy.

If there are conflicts between the breeder's recommendations regarding feeding and health care with those of the veterinarian, discuss these concerns with the breeder. Again, breed-specific knowledge should be carefully considered. In some instances, this may mean obtaining another independent opinion.

In addition to the breeder and veterinarian, there are other resources. The nearest regional Bernese Mountain Dog club is an excellent choice for information. Bernerfolk have had a wonderful network of caring connections long before the advent of the Internet. The local all-breed and obedience clubs will be able to assist with directing you to training classes. Not to be forgotten are a wealth of books available by experts in their fields. The Internet can be very helpful, but it is open to the informed as well as the "instant expert." In every case, always evaluate the qualifications of whatever resource you are using.

chapter 5

Feeding
Your **Bernese**
Mountain Dog

Canine nutrition has long been a subject of debate. There is constant research concerning diet, particularly as it pertains to pet health issues. Added to this is the high profile advertising done by the numerous dog food companies as well as the various lines of products offered within each single company. As a result, choosing the right dog food becomes very confusing.

The best selection of the most advanced commercial foods is at stores specializing in pet food and care products. Dietary information from experienced owners and breeders, based upon personal success with their own dogs, is also worthwhile. The following sections on feeding should prove helpful in making knowledgeable decisions in feeding your Berner.

What Type of Food to Select

5

5

The basic dog food offerings are dry, semi-moist, and canned. The best choice for a Berner is dry food in the form of a well-balanced, premium-quality kibble, prepared with natural preservatives. In meeting the nutritional needs of a large breed, kibble provides your dog with necessary bulk and chewing satisfaction. The specific formula of kibble to select for a Bernese Mountain Dog is usually based upon age. You might also choose a formulation specifically for large breeds. Semi-moist and canned dog foods are not suited to providing the bulk and nutritional needs of a Berner.

Most Berners need little persuasion to eat. If anything, they are usually in need of careful monitoring to prevent excessive weight gain. For those rare times when he is off his feed, a very small amount of meaty, canned food or cottage cheese may be added on a temporary basis to encourage eating.

Taking the attitude that 'nothing is too good for my Berner' should dictate a willingness to pay for the highest quality kibble, but it should not extend to "beefing" up the food with canned, fresh, or home-cooked meat as this can create an imbalanced diet to the detriment of skeletal growth and maintenance.

TYPES OF FOODS/TREATS

There are three types of commercially available dog food—dry, canned and semi-moist—and a huge assortment of treats (lucky dogs!) to feed your dog. Which should you choose?

Dry and canned foods contain similar ingredients. The primary difference between them is their moisture content. The moisture is not just water. It's blood and broth, too—the very things that dogs adore—making canned food more palatable. However, dry food is more economical, convenient and effective in controlling tartar buildup. Just be sure your dog is getting the nutrition he needs (you and your veterinarian can determine this).

Semi-moist foods have the flavor dogs love and the convenience owners want. However, they tend to contain excessive amounts of artificial colors and preservatives.

Dog treats come in every size, shape and flavor imaginable, from organic cookies shaped like postmen to beefy chew sticks. Dogs seem to love them all, so enjoy the variety. Just be sure not to overindulge your dog. Factor treats into his regular meal sizes.

Feeding the Berner Puppy

Before bringing your puppy home, inquire about the feeding schedule, amounts, and brand of food the puppy is used to. Try to have this same food on hand before getting the puppy. If this isn't possible, request a couple of day's worth of food when you pick up your puppy to tide you over until you can purchase the same brand. If the recommended brand is not available, select a food with a similar content analysis. Gradually, make the transition to the different food over a period of several days by adding a small portion of the new food to some of what the puppy has been eating all along. A sudden shift in diet may cause diarrhea or disinterest in an unfamiliar food.

It is very probable that for the first few days the puppy will not eat all the prescribed meal allotment in the absence of competition from litter mates and the newness of surroundings. Since litter feeding does not lend itself to restricting amounts, your teddy-bear chubby Berner puppy may benefit by slimming down a bit.

The opportunity to eat at each meal should be limited to 15 to 20 minutes. This time should be free of distraction or interference by other pets or children. At the end of that time, pick up and discard the food. This should become your dog's lifetime routine.

This owner has carefully measured her puppy's kibble. Every dog will not require the same amount of food, so adjust your dog's portions gradually until you hit upon the right quantity.

Due to the accelerated growth of Bernese Mountain Dog puppies, many breeders feel that puppies being fed regular puppy kibble should be gradually switched to adult kibble starting at about 16 weeks of age. The protein level of the adult food should range between 21% to 26% with the fat level ranging between 12% to 15%. The rationale is to slow down a puppy's growth rate in an effort to deter skeletal problems. If a puppy is being fed a large-breed puppy food formulated to slow rapid growth, follow the manufacturer's age recommendations when switching to adult food.

An 8-week-old puppy is usually fed three times a day. Depending upon the size of the puppy, he will need 1 to 1½ cups of kibble per meal. Slightly soften the food with warm water unless the breeder stipulates dry feeding.

How much to increase the amount of food offered at each meal is almost impossible to generalize due to differences in the size, energy, and metabolism of each puppy. Amounts given on dog food bags should not be used as a guide because these are far too excessive for the typical Berner. Increases in quantity should be very gradual. While cute, being roly-poly is not in the Berner puppy's best interests and is definitely not the criteria for healthy growth. A puppy should be lean, not bulging, and you should feel a slight narrowing at the "waist," that area between the ribs and the hips, when running both hands down the sides of your puppy. Overall growth should be slow and steady.

At about 5 to 6 months of age your Berner may be reduced to two meals per day and eventually reduced to one meal per day unless it is feasible to continue feeding two smaller meals twice daily. If feeding once daily, a dog biscuit given at the time of the discontinued meal makes a nice snack.

Supplements

The addition of nutritional supplements creates an imbalance in the diet. The major concerns are increased growth rate and overstimulation of bone growth that may lead to skeletal problems.

Some breeders feel very strongly that vitamin C should be added to the diet because of its function in the formation of bones, joint cartilage, and ligaments as well as its benefits as an antioxidant. Because vitamin C is water-soluble

---

TO SUPPLEMENT OR NOT TO SUPPLEMENT?

If you're feeding your dog a diet that's correct for his developmental stage and he's alert, healthy-looking and neither over- nor underweight, you don't need to add supplements. These include table scraps as well as vitamins and minerals. In fact, unless you are a nutrition expert, using food supplements can actually hurt a growing puppy. For example, mixing too much calcium into your dog's food can lead to musculoskeletal disorders. Educating yourself about the quantity of vitamins and minerals your dog needs to be healthy will help you determine what needs to be supplemented. If you have any concerns about the nutritional quality of the food you're feeding your dog, discuss them with your veterinarian.

with unused amounts passing from the system, there is no risk of harmful build-up. You can use the same type of vitamin C as is taken by humans. However, do not get chewable tablets as the flavors are not palatable to dogs. Recommended daily dosage, based upon weight, is as follows:

Up to 25 pounds—250 mg.

Over 25 pounds—500 mg.

Over 50 pounds—1000 mg.

If possible, divide the 500 and 1000 mg. dosages in half then give the smaller dosages twice daily. The tablets may be wrapped in cream cheese, peanut butter, or cheese spread and placed on top of your dog's food.

Feeding the Adult Berner

While dogs can generally be considered adults at 1 year of age, a Berner is not fully grown until he is 18 months to 2 years of age. The same premium quality, naturally preserved adult kibble of 21% to 26% protein and 12% to 15% fat that he started eating at about four months of age is still an excellent choice. A total of four cups of food per day is usually adequate for all but the largest males who may need five cups.

Some Berners do well with dry food, enjoying the crunchiness. For those that wolf their food, mixing the food with warm water will be more filling and keep them from swallowing air. The risk of bloat or gastric torsion is also lessened by

---

HOW TO READ THE DOG FOOD LABEL

With so many choices on the market, how can you be sure you are feeding the right food to your dog? The information is all there on the label—if you know what you're looking for.

Look for the nutritional claim made up front. Is the food "100% nutritionally complete"? If so, it's for nearly all life stages; "growth and maintenance," on the other hand, is for early development. Puppy foods and foods for senior dogs are specially marked so you can choose the proper food for your dog's life stage.

Ingredients are listed in descending order by weight. The first three or four ingredients will tell you the bulk of what the food contains. Look for the highest-quality ingredients, like meats and grains, to be among them.

The Guaranteed Analysis tells you what levels of protein, fat, fiber and moisture are in the food, in that order. While these numbers are meaningful, they won't tell you much about the quality of the food.

In many ways, seeing is believing. If your dog has bright eyes, a shiny coat, a good appetite and a good energy level, chances are his diet's fine. Your dog's breeder and your veterinarian are good sources of advice if you're still not sure which food is appropriate.

slightly softening the food with water and by feeding two smaller meals per day instead of one. (see Chapter 7, "Bloat")

Feeding the Spayed or Neutered Berner

Close monitoring of weight is particularly necessary if your Berner has been spayed or neutered. With the increasing trend to spay or neuter at very early ages, the tendency to put on extra pounds brought about by neutering or spaying can lead to and/or exacerbate developmental disorders in a growing puppy. A Berner should be growing up, not out!

While the older, spayed or neutered Berner with a weight problem might benefit by one of the "lite" diets, the most effective control is in reduced amounts of food with snacks of low-cal veggies.

The Geriatric Berner

As with people, the visible effects of aging vary. An active Berner who gets plenty of exercise and is energetically involved in doing things with his master will appear physically younger than his sedentary counterpart. Your veterinarian will be helpful in assessing whether your 7- or 8-year-old Berner should be placed on a diet of food designed for older dogs. Some of these contain nutritional supplements, such as glucosamine and chondroitin sulfate, that are beneficial to those dogs suffering from arthritis.

Even though your Bernese Mountain Dog will eat with gusto, it is best to make sure she doesn't overeat.

Water

The importance of having fresh, cool water available both inside and outside cannot be emphasized enough. Kibble, even when mixed with water, must be fed with access to plenty of water, not only at feeding time but at all times. This access to water may be limited after the final night walk before going to bed, particularly during the period of house-breaking. Water bowls and buckets should be rinsed at each filling and washed with soap and water once daily.

If you have a water softening system or use bottled water for your own consumption, your Berner should also have bottled water for drinking and mixing with dry food. When traveling, bring water from home or purchase good quality bottled water to prevent intestinal upsets due to change in water.

Your Bernese Mountain Dog should always have plenty of fresh drinking water available.

Treats

Nothing stimulates quick training like a treat. It is easy for these rewards to become frequent enough to equal a mini-meal. For that reason, it is a good idea to have two types of treats, one bite-size treat for a tidbit "thank you," and the other, a larger, balanced-diet biscuit for snacks. There are numerous commercial brands from which to select.

Since many Berners enjoy fruits and vegetables, any that appeal to your Berner will make healthy treats. Introduction to broccoli, carrots, apples, seedless grapes, bananas, and melon balls may start at 3 to 4 months of age. Your Berner will treat some of these munchies with disdain while others will be savored. Don't develop these taste buds unless you are prepared to indulge your Berner's appetite for fruit and vegetable treats.

Feeding treats from the table is a habit that should never be started. Most families find the presence of their Berner in the dining area a pleasant addition, but the begging Berner is a nuisance. One well-mannered Berner quietly maintained his post at the table next to the baby's highchair, unobtrusively keeping the carpet spotless.

Chocolate should never be fed to dogs. Excess can even cause death. Treats or toys that are artificially flavored with chocolate should be avoided as they will acquaint your Berner with its smell and taste. Children need to be cautioned against sharing food with the dog and carelessness with candy, particularly at those times of year when quantities may be in the house.

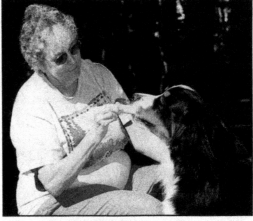

Treats help you and your Berner along with the training process.

TABLE SCRAPS

Emphasis has been placed on the need for a balanced diet. Table scraps do not contribute to this concept. Additionally, these inconsistent, mystery meals, whether offered separately or as a mixer, can cause an upset stomach with temporary diarrhea and vomiting. Table scraps are definitely not appropriate for puppies. If the temptation to share leftover bounty from the table or restaurant with an adult Berner cannot be resisted, keep fat to a bare minimum. Meat should always be cut off bones, even from the thickest prime rib. Such bones can splinter and become impacted in the gums, throat, or digestive tract. You'll soon discover your Berner's tolerance for these occasional, dietary escapades that may not be worth the risk of his getting sick. The safest route is the garbage disposal, despite your Berner's desire to replace it.

Monitoring Weight

Maintaining your Berner in good, healthy weight is a life-long commitment. With maturity, weight will stabilize, but he will continue to need regulation to maintain his energy requirements based upon age and activity.

chapter 6

Grooming

Your **Bernese**

Mountain Dog

The picture-perfect beauty of the Bernese Mountain Dog needs no special enhancements to make a special impression. With her all-occasion black, rust and white outfit, the Berner attracts attention wherever she goes. Keeping a Bernese Mountain Dog's appearance in tiptop shape requires minimal effort. Berners are a "natural" breed, meaning their appearance is not created artificially through grooming as are some breeds, such as Poodles. The coat, with its bright natural sheen as described in the standard, is virtually self-cleaning. Periodic brushing and an occasional bath make "do it yourself" grooming of the Bernese Mountain Dog quite simple.

By starting regular, routine maintenance when a puppy is young, she will soon look forward to grooming sessions as a special time reserved just for her. The baby Berner should be lightly brushed daily, whether she needs it or not, to acquaint her with this experience. Always end by telling her how pretty she looks. Daily brushing may be gradually reduced to every other day and then to once weekly, unless conditions dictate otherwise, such as seasonal shedding.

A secondary, but equally important, benefit of "hands-on" grooming is giving your Berner a checkup of her physical well-being. It should be a routine appraisal of skin, coat, eyes, ears, and teeth. Your hands will become accustomed to how your Berner should feel to the touch. This valuable information will enable you to detect changes that may need attention.

Basic Tools

Purchasing quality products may seem expensive at first, but it is cheaper in the long run. Wholesale pet supply catalogs offer a wide selection and price range. However, being able to look at and feel the product at a local store is always nice.

Daily brushing acclimates your puppy to grooming.

BRUSHES AND COMBS

The beginning needs for a Berner puppy are a stiff, natural bristle brush with a comfortable handle and a stainless steel or nickel-plated comb. Some prefer a comb with a handle while others choose a long comb with a combination of medium/coarse teeth. A slicker brush is not recommended for use on the puppy's short, wooly coat as its steel bristles easily penetrate the

coat, allowing them to scratch and aggravate tender skin. Management of the adult coat is best achieved

63

with the following: a large pin brush; a stiff, natural bristle brush; a soft slicker brush; a sturdy comb with a combination of medium/coarse teeth; and a comb with rotating teeth. Pin brushes are available with steel, ball tips that eliminate the risk of scratching the skin.

NAIL CLIPPERS

Although dog and master dislike this aspect of grooming, it is vastly better than offensive long nails, which on a puppy, can be quite sharp. Select a nail trimmer that has a safety bar that keeps the nail at a safe cutting length. This type is preferred over the guillotine style clipper that does not have that feature. Styptic powder to stop bleeding is a good accessory to have on hand in the event of cutting a nail too short.

SCISSORS

A pair of good quality grooming shears is needed to trim the hair between the pads and around the feet of the adult Berner. If at all possible, choose blunt-tipped

Brushing your Berner's coat produces beautiful results.

scissors to avoid poking your Berner with the sharp point of most shears. A pair of 4-inch round tip, hair cutting scissors will do this job adequately.

Brushing

The purpose of brushing is to allow air to get to the skin, to distribute the coat's natural oils, and to remove dust, foreign particles, and dead hair. It is also the time to examine the skin and check for external parasites. Done daily for the puppy as a part of training and at least weekly for the adult, this task will be greatly simplified by elevating your Berner to a more manageable height to reduce your bending over. A picnic table or bench works well. Assist your dog in getting on and off the table or bench. Great care must be taken that the puppy doesn't fall or jump off. Jumping down from table height is much too stressful a landing for the front assembly of the dog. Ease her down or teach her to use a bench as a step. Some owners prefer sitting on the floor with their Berner.

Start with the front of the chest, brushing the coat upward in the opposite direction of the coat's natural lay. The choice of brush will depend upon length and density of the hair. The bristle brush works well on the shorter coated dog and on the short coat of the legs. The pin brush may be needed to penetrate more deeply. Brush the short hair of the legs against the lay of the hair, finishing with downward brushing. Leg feathering should be combed and brushed as well. From there, work your way up and around the head. The hair behind the ears should be brushed and checked with a comb and your fingers to be sure there are no tangles. Proceed along the sides and the back over the rump to the base of the tail, brushing the hair toward the front of the dog. The hair on the hind legs should be brushed upwards, with the short hair being treated the same as for the front. The back of the hocks should be brushed upwards with the slicker brush and/or comb and then smoothed. If this hair is excessively long, it can be trimmed while brushed upwards to reveal actual length. After this hair is brushed downwards, it will not look like it has been trimmed. Thinning shears are useful for this process should trimming be necessary.

Believe it or not, a picnic table is the perfect accessory for grooming your Berner.

The thick, long hair of the tail and backs of the thighs are best managed with a pin brush. Use a downward stroke on the backs of the thighs, being sure to include brushing the inside of the legs. The tail is the most difficult to do as most Berners object to it being grasped and brushed, particularly when dealing with the underside of the tail. A trick that usually works is to bring the tail around the thigh, brushing it as it lays against the body. Another method is to brush the tail when the dog is lying down.

Shedding

Breeders often refer to shedding as "blowing coat." During a shedding period, brushing will need to be vigorous and daily to hasten the process. A curved slicker does a commendable job of ridding the coat of clumps of hair that develop with a full blown shed. This is the time when you will need to use the full arsenal of brushes and combs.

Because shedding normally coincides with hot weather, it is a favor to your Berner to expedite the process by frequent brushing. A bath is also a favor to your Berner; it will also be followed by heavy-duty shedding. Some prefer bathing to hasten things along. However, don't even consider shaving the coat to solve the problems of heat and shedding. Such an intrusion negates the centuries-old natural ability of the Berner's coat to manage changes in temperature.

HEIDI AND THE VACUUM

From puppyhood, Heidi, a Berner in a super-tidy home, was introduced to light grooming with the vacuum cleaner's upholstery tool. Her mistress acquainted Heidi with the vacuum over a period of days, sitting down on the floor while playing with her with the cleaner off and then running. With the vacuum off, the upholstery attachment was stroked down Heidi's back. Finally, with suction on low, it was gently moved over her back, with care being taken to avoid the ears. Later the suction was increased. Soon Heidi was standing for full-body vacuuming. The only problem was that Heidi now appeared everytime the vacuum was pulled from the closet, insisting upon her "massage."

Ears

Because the drop ears of Bernese Mountain Dogs do not permit the circulation of air, it is important to clean them routinely. Once weekly is usually adequate to maintain healthy ears. Ear cleaning pads for dogs, pre-treated with anti-bacterial and anti-fungal agents, are excellent for regular maintenance. Always use gentle, upward strokes as you clean a short distance into the ear canal. Use a fresh pad for each ear. Finish by wiping the inside of the flap until it is clean. It is much easier to maintain healthy ears than it is to wait for signals that something is wrong. If your Berner unduly scratches her ears, groans when you pet her ears, or frequently shakes her head, veterinary intervention may be necessary (see Chapter 7, "Ear Mites").

Eyes

Inspection of your Berner's beautiful eyes requires no effort because you look into them so many times a day. They should be clear and bright. Wipe away any discharge with a soft tissue. If the eyes are irritated by dust, pollen, or wind, a few drops of any brand of natural tears for

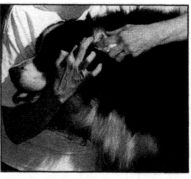

If you are gentle when cleaning your dog's ears, she'll come to love the extra attention.

humans will flush them. Swollen lids and excessive tearing may indicate gnat bites—a temporary problem—or entropion, a more serious, persistent condition. Droopy, lower eyelids that become reddened easily may indicate ectropion (see Chapter 7, "Entropion, Ectropion").

Nails

Keeping the nails trimmed regularly begins as a puppy. It is not the easiest task and may at first require the assistance of a helper and a biscuit to keep the puppy entertained. Objection to nail clipping is almost always the result of the quick having been cut. If you are inexperienced in cutting nails, ask the breeder or

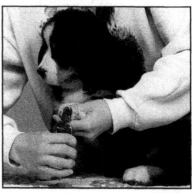

When trimming nails, as with all aspects of grooming, start when your puppy is young.

veterinarian to show you how. Berners have white and black toenails. The quick can be identified in the white nails as the darker pink area. Nip off the nail tip without cutting into the pink part. By locating how much distance there is between the tip of the nail and quick on the white nails, you can approximate how much to clip off on those that are black. It is better to cut too little than too much. No matter how careful you are, the quick may be cut, resulting in bleeding. That can be stopped with styptic powder or stick.

While puppy nails do need clipping to keep them short, most Berners, as they grow older, wear their nails down to an acceptable length during exercise on sidewalks, pavement, and dirt paths. Nonetheless, monitor and clip nails as needed to keep them short without waiting for the annual visit to the veterinarian. Neglected toenails click on the floor, look unsightly, and inflict painful scratches.

Teeth

Oral hygiene is as important to your dog's health as it is to your own.

It is important to inspect your Berner's teeth and gums when grooming. The gums should be pink and the teeth pearly white. When your puppy starts to shed his baby teeth, check the canines (the eye teeth) weekly. If

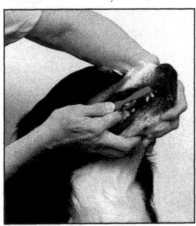

the baby canines are sharing the same space along side the adult canines, ask your veterinarian whether assistance is needed in their removal.

For a healthy mouth, canine toothpastes can be used with a special brush or treated pads to clean your Berner's teeth. Start regular teeth cleaning procedures a few days after your puppy has settled into her new home. Start by sitting down on the floor and holding your puppy beside you. By being patient and brief, she'll think it's a game. Soon, this will be a pleasant routine.

Bathing

When and how often to bathe depends upon what your dog is doing and your personal preference. For the first reason, it is a good idea to keep some dog shampoo on hand for the unexpected. Barring that, the self-cleaning nature of the Bernese Mountain Dog coat, assisted by routine brushing, really reduces the need for bathing. But, one particularly good time to bathe your Berner is when she starts to shed.

Select a good quality shampoo specifically formulated for dogs. Since human shampoos have a different pH, they should not be used, nor should liquid dishwashing soap. Most veterinary offices have a good selection of shampoos for a variety of needs: dry skin, medicated, flea/tick, etc. An insecticidal shampoo is really not necessary and may even be contra-indicated if your Berner is on a regimen of external or internal prevention for fleas and/or ticks. A medicated shampoo is often a good choice as it is usually designed to fight dandruff and relieve dry skin, two common problems for house dogs. If taking your dog to a professional groomer, discuss the type of shampoo that will be used.

> ## QUICK AND PAINLESS NAIL CLIPPING
>
> This is possible if you make a habit out of handling your dog's feet and giving your dog treats when you do. When it's time to clip nails, go through the same routine, but take your clippers and snip off just the end of the nail—clip too far down and you'll cut into the "quick," the nerve center, hurting your dog and causing the nail to bleed. Clip two nails a session while you're getting your dog used to the procedure, and you'll soon be doing all four feet quickly and easily.

Prior to bathing, thoroughly brush your Berner and clean her ears. When finished, wash the brushes and combs so they will be ready for the next time. Gather shampoo, a wash cloth, cotton balls, and several large towels before starting the bath. A super absorbent cloth for drying is now on the market and available at pet and automotive stores. Check the shampoo to determine if it is concentrated and requires diluting with water. A thoroughly rinsed liquid dishwashing soap container is excellent if dilution is required because it has a handy controlled dispenser.

Just before starting the bath, plug your Berner's ears with cotton to prevent water from entering. The eyes may be protected from soap by putting in a few drops of mineral oil. Even so, take care to keep soap out of them. Have your Berner on a web leash and chain choke to keep her in place. A leather leash may leak color, and it will lose its suppleness upon drying after having been saturated with soap and water. When drawing the bath water, carefully regulate the temperature so that it's warm, not hot.

Wet your dog thoroughly working from front to back, starting just behind the ears and going clear around the neck ruff. By leaving her head and ears as the last to wet and shampoo, your dog does not begin the bath with

This puppy loves getting her bath. Her owner is careful to use shampoo specially formulated for dogs.

the unpleasant and upsetting experience of water on the face and the tickling sensation of water touching the insides of her ears.

Apply the shampoo around the neck ruff just behind the ears to form a circular barrier to prevent the migration of fleas. You'll need to keep wetting your dog as you move from front to back due to the waterproof nature of the Bernese coat. Shampoo down the "shirtfront" and under the chest, up and down the legs, under the armpits, then down the back and sides working it deep into the coat. With the soapy washcloth and more shampoo scrub the belly and underparts. Lather hindlegs, inside and out, the tail, and the long rear skirt. Wash in between the toes on each foot. Be sure the entire body has been shampooed. Use plenty of water to get the shampoo to lather.

It is now time to return to the head and ears. Apply shampoo to head and muzzle, working around the eyes. Use the wash cloth to wash and clean the face. Because of the natural oil of the ears, they should be well-lathered, including the lower inside earflaps.

Start rinsing from the neck ruff to the tail, leaving the freshly lathered head until last so that the shampoo has time to work. Return to the head and ears using your hand to shield the eyes. Take particular care not to let water pour into the ears as you rinse them. The cotton plugs will help to prevent major penetration. At this point, expect a good shaking to saturate you and the surroundings. If the cotton balls shake free, put in fresh, dry cotton. Do not reinsert wet cotton. Continue rinsing the rest of your dog until the water is free of any soapy residue. Check by feeling the "shirtfront," neck, ears, and other areas of thick hair. For good measure, give a final rinse covering the head, body, underparts, and pads of feet once more to be sure all shampoo has been removed.

Getting the Berner Dry

Shake, shake, and more shake will rid the coat of surface water. Remove the cotton plugs from the ears if they have not already flipped out. Keep your Berner on a leash or she will resort to rubbing her body repeatedly on whatever surface is available, which is the canine's solution for drying! Starting with the head, carefully dry the inside of the ears. Continue the process by vigorously rubbing her upper and lower body with towels or special water absorbent towels. If possible, take her to a sunny area to trot with you to let her shake and continue drying. Use a brush to fluff the hair. A hair dryer works well, especially for a puppy, but take care not to let it get too hot.

After a bath, eyes and ears need special attention. Your Berner cannot tell you that her eyes burn, so put a few drops of natural tear solution into each eye. The ears, even if kept as dry as possible, should be freshly wiped with an ear cleansing pad because these pads contain drying agents. There are also special drying solutions/powders that are ideal.

All clean!

When your Berner is dry, it is important to give her a good brushing to remove loose hair and any tangles behind the ears. Always use clean brushes and combs.

Optional Trimming

As has been emphasized, Berners are a natural breed. However, there are three areas in which the adult dog can be made more manageable, comfortable and attractive by trimming. These areas are the feet, hocks and ear feathering.

On a mature Berner, the hair between the paw pads can be quite thick, picking up dirt or packing with snow and forming ice balls. This hair can be trimmed out and the long guard hairs growing beyond the nails of the feet can be cut back following the contour of the foot. Use ball tipped grooming shears.

Mr. DeMille, I'm ready for my close-up!

If keeping the long, thick hair behind the ears free of tangles or mats tends to be a problem, carefully scissor out some of the hair in back of the ears. Single-edged thinning shears are particularly useful for this process and they leave a more natural appearance after the trimming, but regular ball tipped grooming shears will do. Always use caution when scissoring around the ears as it is very easy to nip them.

Picture Perfect

The appearance and condition of your Berner are truly a measure of her importance to you. Routine grooming will keep her huggably beautiful and you aware of her external health. With little effort she will always be camera-ready.

chapter 7

Keeping Your Bernese Mountain Dog Healthy

With William N. Spofford, D.V.M.

There is much more to a lifetime of good health than the prerequisite of starting with a bright-eyed Berner puppy from a healthy litter. Some hereditary health problems do not manifest themselves until later. For this reason, it is important to check the genetic health background of your prospective puppy.

So that your Berner will have the optimum chance for being free of the disabling skeletal defects associated with many large-breed dogs, the parents of the litter should be certified free of hip and elbow dysplasia. This extends to grandparents and as many additional generations as possible. The more dogs in a pedigree that are certified clear, the better.

73

Although rare in Bernese Mountain Dogs, PRA (progressive retinal atrophy), which causes eventual blindness, has been identified in the breed. Conscientious breeders are taking a precautionary position by having their breeding stock certified annually with CERF (Canine Eye Registration Foundation).

The ability to certify the condition of breeding stock regarding hips, elbows, and eyes, allows concerned breeders to readily use this valuable information to make the best decisions possible in their breeding programs. By securing these clearances, a breeder can better assure you of a healthy future for your Berner puppy. Nonetheless, it is important to realize that problems can still occur. This is all the more reason for starting out with as strong a background for physical soundness as is possible.

A final component for a happy, healthy Berner puppy is for him to have been bred from quality stock with sound mental health. Just as there are registries for physical health, there are also competitive titles that dogs can earn that are testimony to their ability to get

An ideal puppy is both mentally and physically sound.

along with people. A pedigree that reveals titles in conformation, obedience, and other areas such as tracking, agility, and drafting are usually indicators of good mental heritage. Dogs that have passed the Therapy Dog International or AKC Canine Good Citizen tests have satisfied specific behavioral requirements in their interaction with people. Of course, your personal observation of one or both parents is also invaluable.

Selecting a Veterinarian

You and your Berner's relationship with his veterinarian is a vital ingredient for wellness. While it is helpful to have a doctor who has had experience with the breed, the essential criteria are genuine interest in your pet, and a clean, well-equipped office that has inhalation anesthesia. Isoflurane and propofol are among the safest currently available. You should have a good feeling about your veterinarian's willingness to listen to your observations about your pet's health. No one knows your Berner like you do, so your input is very important. Ask about the diagnostic capabilities as well as the surgical, medical and anesthetic facilities the hospital has to offer. In the event of an unexpected medical crisis, it is essential to have a veterinary hospital with emergency service or referral to a location that is acceptably nearby.

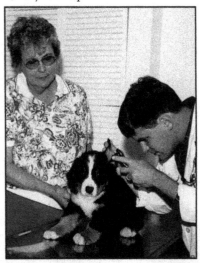

Both you and your Berner should have a good working relationship with your vet.

VETERINARY VISITS

When going to the veterinarian, keep your Berner on a leash and under control. Remember to bring a fecal sample and a list of your questions, symptoms, and any supplies you may need. Going to the veterinarian should be made as pleasant an experience as possible for your Berner. Routine puppy visits to complete the immunization schedule are an ideal opportunity to promote this feeling. A Berner is usually a big hit with the staff. This is a great time to let him be the center of attention. When visiting the veterinarian, be sure to keep your pet away from other dogs and do not permit him to sniff others, the floor, or ground to prevent exposure to sick animals that are there or have been there.

Vaccinations

Thanks to a growing list of vaccines that provide immunization against several highly contagious, often deadly diseases, your Berner can be protected from them. Basic protection begins with a series of vaccinations

75

against **distemper, hepatitis, adenovirus cough, parain-fluenza, parvovirus, coronavirus** and **leptospirosis.** The combination vaccines, commonly referred to as **DHLPPC,** are administered in a single shot that is repeated at specified intervals over a period of several weeks. This is because the puppy has received from her mother antibodies against these diseases. This "natural" immunity counteracts vaccination. At some point between 6 and 16 weeks that "natural" immunity wears off allowing the vaccines to take effect. It is for this reason that it is paramount to adhere to the vaccination schedule followed by annual boosters.

This Berner puppy behaves herself while the veterinarian examines her eyes. A good relationship with the veterinarian ensures pleasant checkups.

A typical schedule of vaccinations is at 6, 9, 12 and 16 weeks. There may be variations in the intervals, with some veterinarians suggesting a booster at 6 months for dogs in high risk areas. Continuing research on the canine immune system results in differing opinions regarding vaccination schedules and boosters. If this becomes an issue of concern for you, discuss it with your veterinarian.

Rabies vaccinations should be given in accordance with state laws, starting usually at 12 or 16 weeks of age. This must be repeated in one year, with subsequent boosters annually or every three years depending upon state laws. If local laws require licensing of pets, proof of rabies vaccination must be furnished. Never postpone rabies vaccination or boosters. It is a red-letter date that cannot be ignored. The seriousness of rabies to the human population is such that an out-of-date vaccination in a situation involving a bite or other exposure, places the very life of your dog in the hands of the local authorities.

Separate immunization against **bordetella,** commonly referred to as **kennel cough,** is a preventive procedure that can spare you and your Berner considerable discomfort and annoyance. Bordetella is characterized by a runny nose and a persistent, gagging cough that often lasts for three weeks. It is highly contagious, passing quickly from dog to dog. Conscientious boarding kennels and training classes require current vaccination. Immunization can be administered as a part of the vaccination schedule.

With the continuing spread of **Lyme disease,** a tickborne bacterial disease, more and more dogs are receiving Lyme vaccine to avoid the possibility of the debilitating and sometimes fatal effects of Lyme disease. Its observable signs may include lameness and swollen joints. Because a young Bernese may exhibit those conditions during growth, it is important to rule out Lyme disease as the source of the problem. Avoidance of ticks can be an effective means of prevention.

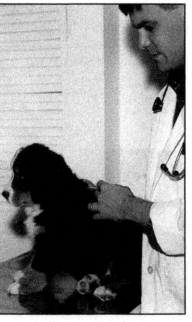

Internal Parasites

Heartworms are transmitted by mosquitoes. It takes only one mosquito to infect a dog. A dog that is infected with heartworms becomes the host. Over a period of time as heartworm disease progresses, an infected dog often develops a chronic cough, experiences weight loss, and becomes exercise intolerant. Diagnosis requires a blood test for the specific detection of heartworms.

Check with your veterinarian to determine the best schedule of vaccinations for your puppy.

While heartworm disease is treatable, the treatment's success is dependent upon the degree of infection, the extent of existing damage to the heart and lungs, and the age and condition of the dog. It is a needless disease when preventive, monthly, oral medication can be obtained from a veterinarian. This should be followed-up with a yearly blood test.

Round, Hook, Whip and Tape Worms are the most common worms that affect dogs. Diagnosis of round, hook, and whipworms is made by microscopic examination of a fecal sample for the presence of eggs. While mature roundworms are sometimes passed with the stool and are visible to the naked eye, hookworms and whipworms are not. These three

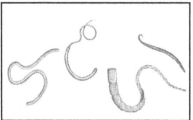

types of worms can be controlled by monthly heartworm preventatives. Tapeworms are not.

The most reliable source of diagnosis of tapeworm infection is visual observation. Egg-carrying

Common internal parasites (l-r): roundworm, whipworm, tapeworm and hookworm.

segments can be seen crawling on the surface of the dog's stool. Because tapeworm infestation is most often caused by ingestion of fleas that have developed from larvae that have fed on tapeworm eggs, the best preventive is effective flea control.

Good sanitation practices cannot be overemphasized enough in controlling intestinal parasites. Stools should be regularly picked up to reduce environmental contamination or reinfection. Disposal should be done in a manner to avoid exposure to other pets, whether your own or someone

Always clean up after your dog—especially in public places.

else's. Fecal pick-up should be considered an obligation, not an option. There is never an okay time to ignore this responsibility.

External Parasites
FLEAS

More than a pesky nuisance, fleas not only serve as a host for tapeworms, they can truly make a dog's life miserable. Some Berners are very sensitive to fleas. As the result of scratching, irritated skin develops crusty lesions that become vulnerable to staph infection.

To detect the presence of fleas, look for their excrement in the form of dark brown particles that look like dirt. This may be found near the dog's rump by parting the hair down to the skin. When rubbed with a dampened paper towel, it will turn reddish brown from the dried blood excreted by the flea. Another prime location is the belly where crawling fleas can sometimes be seen. Since fleas do not spend all of their time on the dog, they can do hit and run damage without being readily detected.

The best thing is to begin flea control management *before* they become a problem. There are several excellent external and internal products available from the veterinarian that are extremely effective in keeping dogs free of fleas. In controlling fleas in the environment, care must be taken in selecting insecticides that are not harmful to animals.

TICKS

Prevention is the key word for protecting your Berner from these blood-sucking parasites that inflict painful, long lasting bites. Also, they can be the carriers of diseases harmful to both dogs and humans. There are some products available from the veterinarian that are effective against both fleas and ticks. Be sure to follow label instructions carefully because there is usually a more frequent application schedule for the prevention of ticks than for fleas.

Even with the use of preventive control, it is important to inspect your Berner after excursions in the woods or

These specks in your dog's fur mean she has fleas.

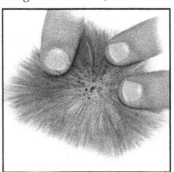

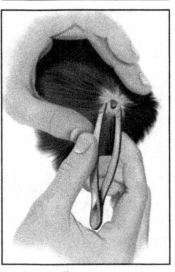

Use tweezers to remove ticks from your dog.

other areas where there may be ticks. Great care should be taken in tick removal so that the head of the tick does not remain to cause further irritation and possible infection. Pour a little alcohol on the tick to get it to loosen its hold. Then grasp the tick with tweezers as close to the skin as possible, pulling the tick away in the direction it is lying. Make every effort to avoid rupturing engorged ticks. Cleanse the area with a chlorhexidine scrub or with anti-bacterial soap and water. Due to the risk of tick-borne disease, do not use bare hands for removal.

EAR MITES

Check your dog regularly for hot spots, especially in summer months.

Repeated scratching of the ears and head shaking may signal the presence of ear mites. Another telltale sign is thick, dark debris that is revealed when cleaning the ears. Since ear mites are not visible to the naked eye, accurate diagnosis and treatment needs to be made by your veterinarian because ear mites must be distinguished from other ear infections. If one pet has ear mites, the others should be inspected by the veterinarian because ear mites spread easily. Cats are particularly suspect and are often overlooked as the source.

Hot Spots

These appear almost overnight or in a matter of hours as an oozing, crusty, and very itchy spot about the size of a quarter that can spread in diameter if untreated. The specific cause is usually unknown, but an irritated flea or tick bite is frequently the precipitator. While hot spots tend to occur in the summer during high humidity, they can appear at any time of year. Typical locations for one of these spots are the back of the neck, the shoulders, and rump. They are not contagious.

Treatment depends a great deal on how quickly the condition is recognized and the extent of the irritated area. The objective is to relieve the itching and to dry up the hot spot. Your veterinarian can provide external and even internal treatments to accomplish this. In treating hot spots, it is important to realize that the painful, frantic itching of a full-blown hot spot can try even the best of temperaments.

Spay/Neuter?

The health benefits by neutering a male or spaying a female to prevent reproduction make this a priority for the Berner as a pet. This applies equally to a puppy designated as pet quality or to a show/breeding quality puppy if the function of the dog will be to serve as a pet. Often a breeder will stipulate a mandatory spay/neuter requirement in selling a puppy as a pet. This restriction would not be made on a show/breeding quality puppy, thereby leaving the decision to the owner. Spaying or neutering are definitely in the best interest of your Berner.

Neutering males prevents testicular cancer and prostate problems. Your Berner's masculine appearance with a massive broad head and heavy coat will be unaffected by neutering. The idea of having a male breed once for the experience is a notion that can backfire. Once introduced to breeding, he will start marking territory and will, most certainly, be interested in females from then on. A decided advantage of neutering is that it makes a more tractable dog. With the absence of certain hormones, he will be much less distracted by his natural, sexual interests. It really contributes to having a very agreeable pet.

ADVANTAGES OF SPAYING/NEUTERING

The greatest advantage of spaying (for females) or neutering (for males) is that you are guaranteed your dog will not produce puppies. There are too many puppies already for too few homes. There are other advantages as well.

ADVANTAGES OF SPAYING

No messy heats.

No "suitors" howling at your windows or waiting in your yard.

No risk of pyometra (disease of the uterus) and decreased incidences of mammary cancer.

ADVANTAGES OF NEUTERING

Decreased incidences of fighting, but does not affect the dog's personality.

Decreased roaming in search of bitches in season.

Decreased incidences of many urogenital diseases.

Spaying females prior to their first heat virtually eliminates the risk of mammary tumors. It also rules out the possibility of pyometra, a serious uterine infection that can cause death. However, the greatest benefit of spaying is the elimination of heat cycles that usually start after 10 months of age in the Bernese Mountain Dog. These re-occur every six to eight months and last about three weeks.

Spaying and neutering decreases the number of unwanted puppies.

Puppies are cute, but breeding is a huge responsibility.

If you are tempted to consider letting your Berner have a litter, be aware that Bernese Mountain Dogs often require Caesarian-sections to deliver their puppies. This is often due to uterine inertia that cannot be determined in advance of delivery. An excessively prolonged whelping process becomes a nightmare when still-borns are produced or worse yet, not produced. At that point veterinary assistance is a priority. Problems with whelping are unpredictable and can vary greatly from litter to litter even from the same mother. There is much joy in having a litter of puppies, but the heartbreaks can be devastating. The decision to breed is best left to those with knowledge and experience in Bernese Mountain Dogs.

Your Berner's Medicine Chest

The single most important item in your Berner's medicine chest is a rectal or digital thermometer and petroleum jelly to act as a lubricant during insertion. To this, add Kaopectate for diarrhea, a betadine-based surgical scrub for superficial cleansing of broken skin or wounds, peroxide (3%) to induce vomiting in some types of poisoning, canine eye wash or a natural tears solution for humans, rubbing alcohol, large gauze pads, and a 2-inch wide roll of self-adhering elastic bandage. Additional items to include for use under the direction of your veterinarian are buffered aspirin (not acetamenophin or ibuprofen) and Benedryl for allergic reactions to bee stings or insect bites. Lastly, a strap-type Velcro muzzle should be available in the tragic event of serious, painful trauma such as a being hit by a car. As with all dogs, even the gentlest of Berners may need restraint to control the natural canine instinct to respond to severe pain by biting.

Prepare a medicine chest in case your precious puppy becomes ill or has a medical emergency.

Administering Medication

The cardinal rule is to complete the full course of *any* prescribed medication for your Berner. The number one cause of treatment failure is stopping medication too soon. Monthly preventives need to be clearly marked on the calendar so that they are not overlooked. Always read and follow label directions. Additionally, be sure that pills are actually swallowed.

Administering pills can be simplified by disguising the tablet in a tasty treat of food, such as peanut butter or cream cheese. From time to time, make such an offering without a pill so that your Berner will be eager to take the tidbit. That way, when it hides a pill, he will take it willingly. If your pet is too sick to be interested in food, open his mouth and put the pill as far back as possible in his mouth. Clamp his jaws closed and stroke his throat until he swallows. A particularly successful trick is to put the pill in a little margarine or cream cheese, and it will practically slide down his throat.

Giving your dog a pill can be easy if you know how.

Liquid medication can be given very easily with an oral syringe. Most likely, your veterinarian will provide you with one if a liquid has been prescribed. If not, ask for one; it will make your job much easier and considerably more pleasant for your Berner.

First Aid

Being prepared for an emergency can save your Berner's life. Some situations can be managed much as you would for a human being. Prompt, careful action is imperative. Try to remain calm. This will be reassuring to your Berner. Important numbers to keep by the telephone are those of your veterinarian, the emergency clinic, and the Poison Control Center.

TEMPERATURE

Monitoring a dog's temperature if you suspect he is ill can provide you with valuable information as to your Berner's condition. This information will also be useful to your veterinarian. Use a rectal or digital thermometer. Lubricate the tip with petroleum jelly and gently insert it about two inches into the anus. Hold onto the thermometer. It should be left in for at least two full minutes. A normal temperature for a dog is 101.5° to 102.5°F.

Diarrhea

An occasional intestinal upset can be expected now and then, just as in humans. Intestinal parasites and sudden changes in diet or water can often precipitate such a bout. Stools that are bloody, watery, and full of mucous signal the need for veterinary consultation, as are recurrent episodes of upset. Diarrhea is of special concern in puppies because they can easily become dehydrated.

Vomiting

As a one-time event, there is usually no cause for concern. If vomiting continues or happens with some predictability under specific conditions, it is time to check with the veterinarian. The presence of blood is a definite signal to get professional help. In some cases where the dog may have ingested toxic or poisonous substances, it may prove useful to your veterinarian if you have collected the vomit in a plastic bag. This action saved one dog's life when portions of a particularly poisonous mushroom were found in the vomit.

A healthy Berner's temperature falls between 101.5° and 102.5°F.

Heatstroke

This is a life-threatening situation that requires immediate action to prevent death. Canine mechanisms for heat relief are panting and sweating through the pads of the feet. That is not a lot of area. Dogs that are experiencing heatstroke have a rapid increase of body temperature (normal range is 101.5° to 102.5°F), heavy panting with labored breathing, and general distress. Rapid cool down is vital. Ideally, get the dog into air conditioning. Apply ice packs to the groin and belly, feet, and head to reduce internal temperature. Putting a fan directly on the dog will assist with cooling. Offer cool water for the dog to drink on his own. If possible, monitor the dog's temperature every 15 minutes. When it starts to drop, discontinue the use of ice packs. Keep the dog as quiet as possible. Continue to check the temperature. A veterinarian should examine the dog immediately.

Common sense management of your Berner during periods of high heat and humidity, particularly when they are prolonged, is the best prevention for this potential killer. Never underestimate the danger of heatstroke conditions in a parked car.

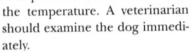

A dog's only cooling mechanisms are panting and sweating through the pads of the feet.

It is important to keep your Bernese Mountain Dog cool, especially on hot days. It looks like these two have found a fun way to beat the heat!

BEE STINGS AND INSECT BITES

Dogs that are allergic to these surprise encounters will experience swelling of the head and face, along with labored breathing. In such an emergency, the oral administration of one Benedryl tablet may bring relief until professional help can be sought. Once an allergic reaction has occurred, it is important to discuss with your veterinarian what to do in the future.

If it appears that your Berner has a broken bone, the risk of further injury must be reduced. Due to pain, the dog may be so frantic that he will bite. For this reason, muzzle him. The muzzle should be firmly secured, but not so tightly as to interfere with breathing. A broken limb should be supported and immobilized as soon as possible. A rolled magazine or newspaper can serve as a makeshift splint to prevent movement. Hold it in place with tape, elastic bandage or strips of cloth. If that is not available, the support of a pillow will help.

Time is of the essence. Transporting an injured, full-grown Berner with minimal motion of his body will be difficult. Gently slide him onto a blanket or sheet so that he can be lifted. If he were put on a board or crate bottom to lift him, he would need to be strapped in place to prevent his jumping or falling off. Alert the veterinary hospital that you are on your way.

ACCIDENTAL POISONING

As soon as you realize that a poisonous or toxic substance has been ingested, there are two valuable resources to tell you what to do. They are your veterinarian and the Poison Control Center. The National Animal Poison Control Center's number (888-426-4435) is a toll free number, but there is a charge for consultation that is made to your credit card or to your phone bill if you prefer to dial a 900 number they can provide. In all instances, give as much information as you can about when and what has been swallowed. If you know what your dog has eaten, be sure to take the container with you when you go to the veterinarian. If that

---

WHEN TO CALL THE VETERINARIAN

In any emergency situation, you should call your veterinarian immediately. Try to stay calm when you call, and give the vet or the assistant as much information as possible before you leave for the clinic. That way, the staff will be able to take immediate, specific action when you arrive. Emergencies include:

- Bleeding or deep wounds
- Hyperthermia (overheating)
- Shock
- Dehydration
- Abdominal pain
- Burns
- Fits
- Unconsciousness
- Broken bones
- Paralysis

Call your veterinarian if you suspect any health problems.

is not available, bring whatever evidence there is, such as leaves, bulbs, etc.

Specific Health Concerns for the Bernese Mountain Dog

CANCER

Documented incidence of cancer in Bernese Mountain Dogs indicates that it is a significant cause of death in the breed. In fact, cancer has become an increasing concern in all dogs, with one out of every four canines being predicted to get some form of cancer. Histiocytosis (malignant and systemic) has been identified as the primary type of cancer that affects Bernese Mountain Dogs. Lymphosarcoma and mast cell tumors are the next most frequent types of cancer. While histiocytosis has been shown to have inherited, familial tendencies, lymphosarcoma does not. Heritability of cancer in Bernese Mountain Dogs is polygenic, meaning multiple genes are involved. Any lumps or masses found on your dog while grooming should be brought to the attention of your veterinarian.

A puppy's love of chewing toys can get him into trouble when it comes to toxic substances.

SKELETAL LAMENESS

Several musculoskeletal disorders may affect rapidly growing, large and giant breeds of dogs. Since Berners are within this category, it is important to understand the most common of these diseases. Visible indicators of a possible problem are lameness and abnormal stance or gait. Veterinary consultation is needed to determine the underlying cause.

Hip Dysplasia

This is a developmental condition affecting the ball and socket joint of the hip that may occur in one or both hips. Hip dysplasia has varying degrees and can only be confirmed by x-ray. Observable signs are lameness in the hindquarters, abnormal gait, and difficulty in getting up from a lying position or negotiating stairs. It is most often noticeable during the first 12 months of life.

While hip dysplasia is hereditary, it is exacerbated by improper diet, obesity, slippery floors, and excessive skeletal stress during the period of rapid growth in the puppy's first year. The extent of discomfort experienced varies a great deal. Although severe cases may require surgical intervention, most dysplastic dogs stabilize and function quite happily. Fortunately, there are medications and nutraceuticals that can alleviate arthritic problems associated with hip dysplasia, particularly in the older dog.

Elbow Dysplasia

This term is used to identify several types of degenerative joint diseases associated with the canine elbow, that point where the upper arm or humerus joins the forearm or ulna. Elbow problems usually develop in young, rapidly growing, large-breed dogs due to joint stress, cartilage development, and irregular bone growth. While injury can result in elbow dysplasia, heredity is considered an important factor in affected dogs. Elbow dysplasia can be exacerbated by obesity and hard landings on the forequarters. Observable signs are limping on the forelegs. As with hip dysplasia, it may be present with no outward signs. Diagnosis requires radiographic examination.

Be on the lookout for breed-specific problems in your puppy.

89

Treatment may require surgical removal of bone fragments to eliminate pain. The same types of medications and nutraceuticals used for managing hips dysplasia may be effective for controlling the discomfort of elbow dysplasia and the resulting arthritic changes.

These days, there are medicines to counteract the effects of arthritis in dogs, so your older Berner can still take part in many of the activities he did as a younger dog.

Osteochondritis Dissecans

Referred to as OCD, this developmental disorder can affect the shoulder, stifle, hock joints, or the elbow. The most common location for OCD is the shoulder. It is characterized by lameness in the affected area and usually occurs during the period of maximum growth between 4 to 8 months. Diagnosis is made by x-ray. Surgical intervention may be required for the dog's comfort. Causal factors include rapid growth, nutritional imbalance, and injury.

Panosteitis

On again, off again lameness that may shift from limb to limb during the ages of 4 to 16 months is most often "Pano." This disease affects young, rapidly growing, large-breed dogs and is frequently the result of an imbalanced diet due to over-supplementation. A slight fever can accompany the initial onset. Veterinary evaluation and guidance in managing this period of canine growing pains is essential because observable signs may be the result of other orthopedic problems.

EYES

Ectropion

Droopy, lower eyelids that roll outwards are ectropic, resulting in reddened eyelids due to irritation by dust and particles. Depending upon the extent of the condition and subjectivity to irritants, flushing the eyes with a few drops of eyewash periodically and after exposure to dusty or windy conditions is usually sufficient for comfort. Although eye infections can occur, ectropion does not damage the dog's vision. Ectropion can be corrected surgically. While this procedure is usually done for cosmetic reasons, it should be considered for dogs having frequent eye infections.

To keep him healthy no matter how much or where he plays, it is important to ensure all of your Berner's vaccinations are up to date.

Entropion

Lower and/or upper eyelids that roll inward are entropic. This defect causes the eyelashes and hairs of the eyelid to brush against the surface of the eye causing continuous pain. The eyes appear puffy, reddened, and teary. Left untreated, this condition may result in permanent damage to the cornea and blindness. Most cases require surgery. Because it is a hereditary defect, dogs so affected should not be used for breeding.

91

UMBILICAL HERNIA IN BERNESE MOUNTAIN DOGS

The presence of an umbilical hernia is rather commonplace in Bernese Mountain Dogs. This is a small protrusion at the navel, midway on the dog's underside where the umbilical cord was attached. It is the result of the umbilical ring not having closed. Due to the high incidence of umbilical hernias in Bernese Mountain Dogs, it is in most cases hereditary. Birth trauma or cutting the cord too close can be a cause. Experience has shown that the need for surgical intervention is indeed rare.

BLOAT OR GASTRIC TORSION

As a large, deep-chested breed, the Bernese Mountain Dog is vulnerable to this life-threatening emergency. Fortunately, its occurrence in Berners is less frequent in comparison with some breeds. Symptoms include repeated, unproductive attempts to vomit, agitation, guarded movement, salivation with panting, and, as it advances, a bloated abdomen. It is usually seen in older dogs. Bloat requires immediate, emergency veterinary attention and usually surgery.

Bloat starts with a rapid build-up of gas and/or fluid in the stomach. The swelling may progress to the point when the stomach actually twists from 90° to 380°, which is torsion. Sometimes this twist occurs when a dog is exercised or is jumping around after consumption of a large meal or a quantity of water.

A FIRST-AID KIT

Keep a canine first-aid kit on hand for general care and emergencies. Check it periodically to make sure liquids haven't spilled or dried up, and replace medications and materials after they're used. Your kit should include:

Activated charcoal tablets to absorb poison

Adhesive tape (1 and 2 inches wide)

Antibacterial ointment (for skin and eyes)

Aspirin (buffered or enteric coated, not Ibuprofen

Bandages: Gauze rolls (1 and 2 inches wide) and dressing pads

Cotton balls

Diarrhea medicine

Dosing syringe

Hydrogen peroxide (3%)

Petroleum jelly

Rectal thermometer

Rubber gloves

Rubbing alcohol

Scissors

Tourniquet

Towel

Tweezers

Precautionary measures to avoid bloat are feeding adults two smaller meals twice daily, moistening the food with water, and delaying strenuous exercise for at least an hour after meals. By keeping fresh water readily available, your Berner will be less inclined to drink large amounts at one time. Unfortunately, once a dog has had bloat, there is the likelihood of recurrence.

Your older Berner may not be as active as he used to be, but he still loves spending time with you.

THE SENIOR BERNER

An old saying by Swiss farmers describes the Berner as, "Three years a young dog, three years a good dog, three years an old dog." To that might be added, "and each year thereafter is a gift." Older dogs, aged 6 and above, need more frequent health checks by the veterinarian. A variety of medications can relieve age-related problems. Good nutrition with weight management, regular exercise, and weekly inspection during grooming for lumps or any other changes in the body will contribute to the good health of your geriatric Berner.

EUTHANASIA

With the commitment of ownership comes the towering responsibility of knowing when to say goodbye. Quality of life must be foremost in making the decision to euthanize your beloved Berner. It requires a full understanding of the health issues. While your veterinarian can present the options, the decision remains with you. The best interests of your Berner must be your guide, not your feelings. Your sense of sorrow and loss at the prospect of being without your pet must become secondary to his needs. The stoic nature of the breed can often mask physical suffering. Those soulful eyes and slow wag of his tail convey the message that everything's all right. It is *you* who must make it right for him.

Your Happy, Healthy Pet

Your Dog's Name _____

Name on Your Dog's Pedigree (if your dog has one) _____
_____

Where Your Dog Came From _____
_____

Your Dog's Birthday _____

Your Dog's Veterinarian

    Name _____

    Address _____

    Phone Number _____

    Emergency Number _____

Your Dog's Health

    Vaccines

        type _____ date given _____

        type _____ date given _____

        type _____ date given _____

        type _____ date given _____

    Heartworm

        date tested _____ type used_____ start date _____

Your Dog's License Number _____

Groomer's Name and Number _____

Dogsitter/Walker's Name and Number _____

Awards Your Dog Has Won

    Award _____ date earned _____

    Award _____ date earned _____

part three

Enjoying

your

Dog

chapter 8

Basic
Training

by Ian Dunbar, Ph.D., MRCVS

Training is the jewel in the crown—the most important aspect of doggy husbandry. There is no more important variable influencing dog behavior and temperament than the dog's education: A well-trained, well-behaved and good-natured puppydog is always a joy to live with, but an untrained and uncivilized dog can be a perpetual nightmare. Moreover, deny the dog an education and it will not have the opportunity to fulfill its own canine potential; neither will it have the ability to communicate effectively with its human companions.

Luckily, modern psychological training methods are easy, efficient and effective and, above all, considerably dog-friendly and user-friendly. Doggy education is as simple as it is enjoyable. But before you can have a good time play-training with your new dog, you have to learn what to do and how to do it. There is no bigger variable influencing the success of dog training than the *owner's* experience and expertise. *Before you embark on the dog's education, you must first educate yourself.*

Basic Training for Owners

Ideally, basic owner training should begin well *before* you select your dog. Find out all you can about your chosen breed first, then master rudimentary training and handling skills. If you already have your puppy/dog, owner training is a dire emergency—the clock is running! Especially for puppies, the first few weeks at home are the most important and influential days in the dog's life. Indeed, the cause of most adolescent and adult problems may be traced back to the initial days the pup explores his new home. This is the time to establish the *status quo*—to teach the puppy/dog how you would like him to behave and so prevent otherwise quite predictable problems.

In addition to consulting breeders and breed books such as this one (which understandably have a positive breed bias), seek out as many pet owners with your breed you can find. Good points are obvious. What you want to find out are the breed-specific *problems*, so you can nip them in the bud. In particular, you should talk to owners with *adolescent* dogs and make a list of all anticipated problems. Most important, *test drive* at least half a dozen adolescent and adult dogs of your breed yourself. An eight-week-old puppy is deceptively easy to handle, but she will acquire adult size, speed and strength in just four months, so you should learn now what to prepare for.

Puppy and pet dog training classes offer a convenient venue to locate pet owners and observe dogs in action. For a list of suitable trainers in your area, contact the Association of Pet Dog Trainers (see Chapter 13). You may also begin your basic owner training by observing other owners in class. Watch as many classes and test drive as many dogs as possible. Select an upbeat, dog-friendly, people-friendly, fun-and-games, puppydog pet training class to learn the ropes. Also, watch training videos and read training books (see Chapter 12). You must find out what to do and how to do it *before* you have to do it.

Principles of Training

Most people think training comprises teaching the dog to do things such as sit, speak and roll over, but even a four-week-old pup knows how to do these things already. Instead, the first step in training involves teaching the dog human words for each dog behavior and activity and for each aspect of the dog's environment. That way you, the owner, can more easily participate in the dog's domestic education by directing him to perform specific actions appropriately, that is, at the right time, in the right place, and so on. Training opens communication channels, enabling an educated dog to at least understand the owner's requests.

In addition to teaching a dog *what* we want her to do, it is also necessary to teach her *why* she should do what we ask. Indeed, 95 percent of training revolves around motivating the dog *to want to do* what we want. Dogs often understand what their owners want; they just don't see the point of doing it—especially when the owner's repetitively boring and seemingly senseless instructions are totally at odds with much more pressing and exciting doggy distractions. It is not so much the dog who is being stubborn or dominant; rather, it is the owner who has failed to acknowledge the dog's needs and feelings and to approach training from the dog's point of view.

The Meaning of Instructions

The secret to successful training is learning how to use training lures to predict or prompt specific behaviors—to coax the dog to do what you want *when* you want. Any highly valued object (such as a treat or toy) may be used as a lure, which the dog will follow with his eyes and nose. Moving the lure in specific ways entices the dog to move his nose, head and entire body in specific ways. In fact, by learning the art of manipulating various lures, it is possible to teach the dog to assume virtually any body position and perform any action. Once you have control over the expression of the dog's behaviors and can elicit any body position or behavior at will, you can easily teach the dog to perform on request.

Tell your dog what you want him to do, use a lure to entice him to respond correctly, then profusely praise

Teach your dog words for each activity he needs to know, like down.

and maybe reward him once he performs the desired action. For example, verbally request "Fido, sit!" while you move a squeaky toy upwards and backwards over the dog's muzzle (lure-movement and hand signal), smile knowingly as he looks up (to follow the lure) and sits down (as a result of canine anatomical engineering), then praise him to distraction ("Gooood Fido!"). Squeak the toy, offer a training treat and give your dog and yourself a pat on the back.

Being able to elicit desired responses over and over enables the owner to reward the dog over and over. Consequently, the dog begins to think training is fun. For example, the more the dog is rewarded for sitting, the more she enjoys sitting. Eventually the dog comes to realize that, whereas most sitting is appreciated, sitting immediately upon request usually prompts especially enthusiastic praise and a slew of high-level rewards. The dog begins to sit on cue much of the time, showing that she is starting to grasp the meaning of the owner's verbal request and hand signal.

Why Comply?

Most dogs enjoy initial lure/reward training and are only too happy to comply with their owners' wishes. Unfortunately, repetitive drilling without appreciative feedback tends to diminish the dog's enthusiasm until he eventually fails to see the point of complying anymore. Moreover, as the dog approaches adolescence he becomes more easily distracted as he develops other interests. Lengthy sessions with repetitive exercises tend to bore and demotivate both parties. If it's not fun, the owner doesn't do it and neither does the dog.

Integrate training into your dog's life: The greater number of training sessions each day and the *shorter* they are, the more willingly compliant your dog will become. Make sure to have a short (just a few seconds) training interlude before every enjoyable canine activity. For example, ask your dog to sit to greet people, to sit before you throw his Frisbee, and to sit for his supper. Really, sitting is no different from a canine "please." Also, include numerous short training interludes during every enjoyable canine pastime, for example, when playing with the dog or when he is running in the park. In this fashion, doggy distractions may be effectively converted into rewards for training. Just as all games have rules, fun becomes training . . . and training becomes fun.

Eventually, rewards actually become unnecessary to continue motivating your dog. If trained with consideration and kindness, performing the desired behaviors will become self-rewarding and, in a sense, your dog will motivate himself. Just as it is not necessary to reward a human companion during an enjoyable walk in the park, or following a game of tennis, it is hardly necessary to reward our best friend—the dog—for walking by our side or while playing fetch. Human company during enjoyable activities is reward enough for most dogs.

Even though your dog has become self-motivating, it's still good to praise and pet him a lot and offer rewards once in a while, especially for a good job well done. And if for no other reason, praising and rewarding others is good for the human heart.

To train your dog, you need gentle hands, a loving heart and a good attitude.

Punishment

Without a doubt, lure/reward training is by far the best way to teach: Entice your dog to do what you want and then reward him for doing so. Unfortunately, a human shortcoming is to take the good for granted and to moan and groan at the bad. Specifically, the dog's many good behaviors are ignored while the owner focuses on punishing the dog for making mistakes. In extreme cases, instruction is *limited* to punishing mistakes made by a trainee dog, child, employee or husband, even though it has been proven punishment training is notoriously inefficient and ineffective and is decidedly unfriendly and combative. It teaches the dog that training is a drag, almost as quickly as it teaches the dog to dislike his trainer. Why treat our best friends like our worst enemies?

Punishment training is also much more laborious and time consuming. Whereas it takes only a finite amount of time to teach a dog what to chew, for example, it takes much, much longer to punish the dog for each and every mistake. Remember, *there is only one right way!* So why not teach that right way from the outset?!

To make matters worse, punishment training causes severe lapses in the dog's reliability. Since it is obviously impossible to punish the dog each and every time she misbehaves, the dog quickly learns to distinguish between those times when she must comply (so as to avoid impending punishment) and those times when she need not comply, because punishment is impossible. Such times include when the dog is off leash and only six feet away, when the owner is otherwise engaged (talking to a friend, watching television, taking a shower, tending to the baby or chatting on the telephone), or when the dog is left at home alone.

Instances of misbehavior will be numerous when the owner is away, because even when the dog complied in the owner's looming presence, he did so unwillingly. The dog was forced to act against his will, rather than moulding his will to want to please. Hence, when the owner is absent, not only does the dog know he need not comply, he simply does not want to. Again, the trainee is not a stubborn vindictive beast, but rather the trainer has failed to teach.

Punishment training invariably creates unpredictable Jekyll and Hyde behavior.

Trainer's Tools

Many training books extol the virtues of a vast array of training paraphernalia and electronic and metallic gizmos, most of which are designed for canine restraint, correction and punishment, rather than for actual facilitation of doggy education. In reality, most effective training tools are not found in stores; they come from within ourselves. In addition to a willing dog, all you really need is a functional human brain, gentle hands, a loving heart and a good attitude.

In terms of equipment, all dogs do require a quality buckle collar to sport dog tags and to attach the leash (for safety and to comply with local leash laws). Hollow chewtoys (like Kongs or sterilized longbones) and a dog bed or collapsible crate are a must for housetraining. Three additional tools are required:

1. specific lures (training treats and toys) to predict and prompt specific desired behaviors;
2. rewards (praise, affection, training treats and toys) to reinforce for the dog what a lot of fun it all is; and
3. knowledge—how to convert the dog's favorite activities and games (potential distractions to training) into "life-rewards," which may be employed to facilitate training.

The most powerful of these is *knowledge*. Education is the key! Watch training classes, participate in training classes, watch videos, read books, enjoy playtraining with your dog, and then your dog will say "Please," and your dog will say "Thank you!"

Housetraining

If dogs were left to their own devices, certainly they would chew, dig and bark for entertainment and then no doubt highlight a few areas of their living space with sprinkles of urine, in much the same way we decorate by hanging pictures. Consequently, when we ask a dog to live with us, we must teach him *where* he may dig and perform his toilet duties, *what* he may chew and *when* he may bark. After all, when left at home alone for many hours, we cannot expect the dog to amuse himself by completing crosswords or watching the soaps on TV!

Also, it would be decidedly unfair to keep the house rules a secret from the dog, and then get angry and punish the poor critter for inevitably transgressing rules he did not even know existed. Remember, without adequate education and guidance, the dog will be forced to establish his own rules—doggy rules—that most probably will be at odds with the owner's view of domestic living.

Since most problems develop during the first few days the dog is at home, prospective dog owners must be certain they are quite clear about the principles of housetraining *before* they get a dog. Early misbehaviors quickly become established as the status quo—

becoming firmly entrenched as hard-to-break bad habits, which set the precedent for years to come. Make sure to teach your dog good habits right from the start. Good habits are just as hard to break as bad ones!

Ideally, when a new dog comes home, try to arrange for someone to be present for as much as possible during the first few days (for adult dogs) or weeks for puppies. With only a little forethought, it is surprisingly easy to find a puppy sitter, such as a retired person, who would be willing to eat from your refrigerator and watch your television while keeping an eye on the newcomer to encourage the dog to play with chewtoys and to ensure he goes outside on a regular basis.

POTTY TRAINING

To teach the dog where to relieve himself:

1. never let him make a single mistake;
2. let him know where you want him to go; and
3. handsomely reward him for doing so: "GOOOOOOOD DOG!!!" liver treat, liver treat, liver treat!

PREVENTING MISTAKES

A single mistake is a training disaster, since it heralds many more in future weeks. And each time the dog soils the house, this further reinforces the dog's unfortunate preference for an indoor, carpeted toilet. *Do not let an unhousetrained dog have full run of the house if you are away from home or cannot pay full attention.* Instead, confine the dog to an area where elimination is appropriate, such as an outdoor run or, better still, a small, comfortable indoor kennel with access to an outdoor run. When confined in this manner, most dogs will naturally housetrain themselves.

If that's not possible, confine the dog to an area, such as a utility room, kitchen, basement or garage, where elimination may not be desired in the long run but as an interim measure it is certainly preferable to doing it all around the house. Use newspaper to cover the floor of the dog's day room. The newspaper may be used to soak up the urine and to wrap up and dispose of the feces. Once your dog develops a preferred spot for eliminating, it is only necessary to cover that part of the floor with newspaper. The smaller papered area may then be moved (only a little each day) towards the door to the outside. Thus the dog will develop the tendency to go to the door when he needs to relieve himself.

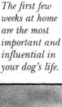

The first few weeks at home are the most important and influential in your dog's life.

Never confine an unhousetrained dog to a crate for long periods. Doing so would force the dog to soil the crate and ruin its usefulness as an aid for housetraining (see the following discussion).

TEACHING WHERE

In order to teach your dog where you would like her to do her business, you have to be there to direct the proceedings—an obvious, yet often neglected, fact of life. In order to be there to teach the dog *where* to go, you need to know *when* she needs to go. Indeed, the success of housetraining depends on the owner's ability to predict these times. Certainly, a regular feeding schedule will facilitate prediction somewhat, but there is

nothing like "loading the deck" and influencing the timing of the outcome yourself!

Whenever you are at home, make sure the dog is under constant supervision and/or confined to a small area. If already well trained, simply instruct the dog to lie down in his bed or basket. Alternatively, confine the dog to a crate (doggy den) or tie-down (a short, 18-inch lead that can be clipped to an eye hook in the baseboard). Short-term close confinement strongly inhibits urination and defecation, since the dog does not want to soil his sleeping area. Thus, when you release the puppydog each hour, he will definitely need to urinate immediately and defecate every third or fourth hour. Keep the dog confined to his doggy den and take him to his intended toilet area each hour, every hour, and on the hour.

When taking your dog outside, instruct him to sit quietly before opening the door—he will soon learn to sit by the door when he needs to go out!

TEACHING WHY

Being able to predict when the dog needs to go enables the owner to be on the spot to praise and reward the dog. Each hour, hurry the dog to the intended toilet area in the yard, issue the appropriate instruction ("Go pee!" or "Go poop!"), then give the dog three to four minutes to produce. Praise and offer a couple of training treats when successful. The treats are important because many people fail to praise their dogs with feeling . . . and housetraining is hardly the time for understatement. So either loosen up and enthusiastically praise that dog: "Wuzzzer-wuzzer-wuzzer, hoooser good wuffer den? Hoooo went pee for Daddy?" Or say "Good dog!" as best you can and offer the treats for effect.

Following elimination is an ideal time for a spot of playtraining in the yard or house. Also, an empty dog may be allowed greater freedom around the house for the next half hour or so, just as long as you keep an eye out to make sure he does not get into other kinds of mischief. If you are preoccupied and cannot pay full attention, confine the dog to his doggy den once more to enjoy a peaceful snooze or to play with his many chewtoys.

If your dog does not eliminate within the allotted time outside—no biggie! Back to his doggy den, and then try again after another hour.

As I own large dogs, I always feel more relaxed walking an empty dog, knowing that I will not need to finish our stroll weighted down with bags of feces! Beware of falling into the trap of walking the dog to get it to eliminate. The good ol' dog walk is such an enormous highlight in the dog's life that it represents the single biggest potential reward in domestic dogdom. However, when in a hurry, or during inclement weather, many owners abruptly terminate the walk the moment the dog has done its business. This, in effect, severely punishes the dog for doing the right thing, in the right place at the right time. Consequently, many dogs become strongly inhibited from eliminating outdoors because they know it will signal an abrupt end to an otherwise thoroughly enjoyable walk.

Instead, instruct the dog to relieve himself in the yard prior to going for a walk. If you follow the above instructions, most dogs soon learn to eliminate on cue. As soon as the dog eliminates, praise (and offer a treat or two)—"Good dog! Let's go walkies!" Use the walk as a reward for eliminating in the yard. If the dog does not go, put him back in his doggy den and think about a walk later on. You will find with a "No feces–no walk" policy, your dog will become one of the fastest defecators in the business.

If you do not have a back yard, instruct the dog to eliminate right outside your front door prior to the walk. Not only will this facilitate clean up and disposal of the feces in your own trash can but, also, the walk may again be used as a colossal reward.

CHEWING AND BARKING

Short-term close confinement also teaches the dog that occasional quiet moments are a reality of domestic living. Your puppydog is extremely impressionable during his first few weeks at home. Regular confinement at this time soon exerts a calming influence over the dog's personality. Remember, once the dog is housetrained and calmer, there will be a whole lifetime ahead for the dog to enjoy full run of the house and garden. On the other hand, by letting the newcomer have unrestricted access to the entire household and allowing him to run willy-nilly, he will most certainly develop a bunch of behavior problems in short order, no doubt necessitating confinement later in life. It would not be fair to remedially restrain and confine a dog you have trained, through neglect, to run free.

When confining the dog, make sure he always has an impressive array of suitable chewtoys. Kongs and sterilized longbones (both readily available from pet stores) make the best chewtoys, since they are hollow and may be stuffed with treats to heighten the dog's interest. For example, by stuffing the little hole at the top of a Kong with a small piece of freeze-dried liver, the dog will not want to leave it alone.

Remember, treats do not have to be junk food and they certainly should not represent extra calories. Rather, treats should be part of each dog's regular daily diet:

Make sure your puppy has suitable chewtoys.

Some food may be served in the dog's bowl for breakfast and dinner, some food may be used as training treats, and some food may be used for stuffing chewtoys. I regularly stuff my dogs' many Kongs with different shaped biscuits and kibble. The kibble seems to fall out fairly easily, as do the oval-shaped biscuits, thus rewarding the dog instantaneously for checking out the chewtoys. The bone-shaped biscuits fall out after a while, rewarding the dog for worrying at the chewtoy. But the triangular biscuits never come out. They remain inside the Kong as lures, maintaining the dog's fascination with its chewtoy. To further focus the dog's interest, I always make sure to flavor the triangular biscuits by rubbing them with a little cheese or freeze-dried liver.

If stuffed chewtoys are reserved especially for times the dog is confined, the puppydog will soon learn to enjoy quiet moments in her doggy den and she will quickly develop a chewtoy habit—a good habit! This is a simple *passive training* process; all the owner has to do is set up the situation and the dog all but trains herself—easy and effective. Even when the dog is given run of the house, her first inclination will be to indulge her rewarding chewtoy habit rather than destroying less-attractive household articles, such as curtains, carpets, chairs and compact disks. Similarly, a chewtoy chewer will be less inclined to scratch and chew herself excessively. Also, if the dog busies herself as a recreational chewer, she will be less inclined to develop into a recreational barker or digger when left at home alone.

Stuff a number of chewtoys whenever the dog is left confined and remove the extra-special-tasting treats when you return. Your dog will now amuse himself with his chewtoys before falling asleep and then resume playing with his chewtoys when he expects you to return. Since most owner-absent misbehavior happens right after you leave and right before your expected return, your puppydog will now be conveniently preoccupied with his chewtoys at these times.

Come and Sit

Most puppies will happily approach virtually anyone, whether called or not; that is, until they collide with

To teach come, call your dog, open your arms as a welcoming signal, wave a toy or a treat and praise for every step in your direction.

adolescence and develop other more important doggy interests, such as sniffing a multiplicity of exquisite odors on the grass. Your mission, Mr. and/or Ms. Owner, is to teach and reward the pup for coming reliably, willingly and happily when called—and you have just three months to get it done. Unless adequately reinforced, your puppy's tendency to approach people will self-destruct by adolescence.

Call your dog ("Fido, come!"), open your arms (and maybe squat down) as a welcoming signal, waggle a treat or toy as a lure, and reward the puppydog when he comes running. Do not wait to praise the dog until he reaches you—he may come 95 percent of the way and then run off after some distraction. Instead, praise the dog's *first* step towards you and continue praising enthusiastically for *every* step he takes in your direction.

When the rapidly approaching puppy dog is three lengths away from impact, instruct him to sit ("Fido, sit!") and hold the lure in front of you in an outstretched hand to prevent him from hitting you midchest and knocking you flat on your back! As Fido decelerates to nose the lure, move the treat upwards and backwards just over his muzzle with an upwards motion of your extended arm (palm-upwards). As the dog looks up to follow the lure, he will sit down (if he jumps up, you are holding the lure too high). Praise the dog for sitting. Move backwards and call him again. Repeat this many times over, always praising when Fido comes and sits; on occasion, reward him.

For the first couple of trials, use a training treat both as a lure to entice the dog to come and sit and as a reward for doing so. Thereafter, try to use different items as lures and rewards. For example, lure the dog with a Kong or Frisbee but reward her with a food treat. Or lure the dog with a food treat but pat her and throw a tennis ball as a reward. After just a few repetitions, dispense with the lures and rewards; the dog will begin to respond willingly to your verbal requests and hand signals just for the prospect of praise from your heart and affection from your hands.

Instruct every family member, friend and visitor how to get the dog to come and sit. Invite people over for a series of pooch parties; do not keep the pup a secret— let other people enjoy this puppy, and let the pup enjoy other people. Puppydog parties are not only fun, they easily attract a lot of people to help *you* train *your* dog. Unless you teach your dog *how* to meet people, that is, to sit for greetings, no doubt the dog will resort to jumping up. Then you and the visitors will get annoyed, and the dog will be punished. This is not fair. *Send out those invitations for puppy parties and teach your dog to be mannerly and socially acceptable.*

Even though your dog quickly masters obedient recalls in the house, his reliability may falter when playing in the back yard or local park. Ironically, it is *the owner* who has unintentionally trained the dog *not* to respond in these instances. By allowing the dog to play and run around and otherwise have a good time, but then to call the dog to put him on leash to take him home, the dog quickly learns playing is fun but training is a drag. Thus, playing in the park becomes a severe distraction, which works against training. Bad news!

Instead, whether playing with the dog off leash or on leash, request him to come at frequent intervals— say, every minute or so. On most occasions, praise and pet the dog for a few seconds while he is sitting, then tell him to go play again. For especially fast recalls, offer a couple of training treats and take the time to praise and pet the dog enthusiastically before releasing him. The dog will learn that coming when called is not necessarily the end of the play session, and neither is it the end of the world; rather, it signals an enjoyable, quality time-out with the owner before resuming play once more. In fact, playing in the park now becomes a very effective life-reward, which works to facilitate training by reinforcing each obedient and timely recall. Good news!

Sit, Down, Stand and Rollover

Teaching the dog a variety of body positions is easy for owner and dog, impressive for spectators and extremely useful for all. Using lure-reward techniques, it is possible to train several positions at once to verbal commands or hand signals (which impress the socks off onlookers).

Sit and *down*—the two control commands—prevent or resolve nearly a hundred behavior problems. For example, if the dog happily and obediently sits or lies down when requested, he cannot jump on visitors, dash out the front door, run around and chase its tail, pester other dogs, harass cats or annoy family, friends or strangers. Additionally, "sit" or "down" are better emergency commands for off-leash control.

It is easier to teach and maintain a reliable sit than maintain a reliable recall. *Sit* is the purest and simplest of commands—either the dog is sitting or he is not. If there is any change of circumstances or potential danger in the park, for example, simply instruct the dog to sit. If he sits, you have a number of options: allow the dog to resume playing when he is safe; walk up and put the dog on leash, or call the dog. The dog will be much more likely to come when called if he has already acknowledged his compliance by sitting. If the dog does not sit in the park—train him to!

Stand and *rollover-stay* are the two positions for examining the dog. Your veterinarian will love you to distraction if you take a little time to teach the dog to stand still and roll over and play possum. Also, your vet bills will be smaller. The rollover-stay is an especially useful command and is really just a variation of the down-stay: whereas the dog lies prone in the traditional down, she lies supine in the rollover-stay.

As with teaching come and sit, the training techniques to teach the dog to assume all other body positions on cue are user-friendly and dog-friendly. Simply give the appropriate request, lure the dog into the desired body position using a training treat or toy and then *praise* (and maybe reward) the dog as soon as he complies. Try not to touch the dog to get him to respond. If you teach the dog by guiding him into position, the dog will quickly learn that rump-pressure means sit, for example, but as yet you still have no control over your dog if he is just six feet away. It will still be necessary to teach the dog to sit on request. So do not make training a time-consuming two-step process; instead, teach the dog to sit to a verbal request or hand signal from the outset. Once the dog sits willingly when requested, by all means use your hands to pet the dog when he does so.

To teach *down* when the dog is already sitting, say "Fido, down!," hold the lure in one hand (palm down) and lower that hand to the floor between the dog's forepaws. As the dog lowers his head to follow the lure, slowly move the lure away from the dog just a fraction (in front of his paws). The dog will lie down as he stretches his nose forward to follow the lure. Praise the dog when he does so. If the dog stands up, you pulled the lure away too far and too quickly.

When teaching the dog to lie down from the standing position, say "down" and lower the lure to the floor as before. Once the dog has lowered his forequarters and assumed a play bow, gently and slowly move the lure *towards* the dog between his forelegs. Praise the dog as soon as his rear end plops down.

After just a couple of trials it will be possible to alternate sits and downs and have the dog energetically perform doggy push-ups. Praise the dog a lot, and after half a dozen or so push-ups reward the dog with a training treat or toy. You will notice the more energetically you move your arm—upwards (palm up) to get the dog to sit, and downwards (palm down) to get the dog to lie down—the more energetically the dog responds to your requests. Now try training the dog in silence and you will notice he has also learned to respond to hand signals. Yeah! Not too shabby for the first session.

To teach *stand* from the sitting position, say "Fido, stand," slowly move the lure half a dog-length away from the dog's nose, keeping it at nose level, and praise the dog as he stands to follow the lure. As soon

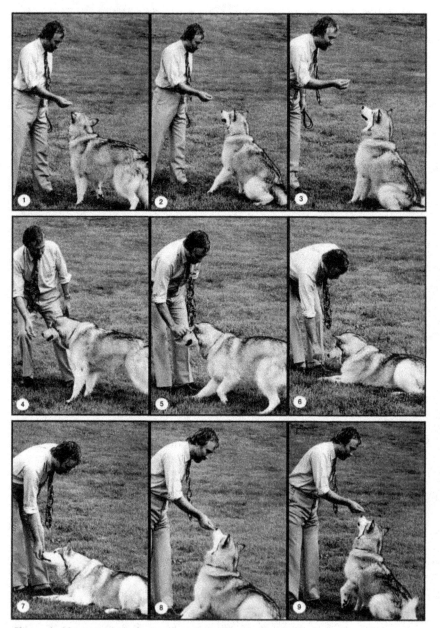

Using a food lure to teach sit, down and stand. 1) "Phoenix, Sit." 2) Hand palm upwards, move lure up and back over dog's muzzle. 3) "Good sit, Phoenix!" 4) "Phoenix, down." 5) Hand palm downwards, move lure down to lie between dog's forepaws. 6) "Phoenix, off. Good down, Phoenix!" 7) "Phoenix, sit!" 8) Palm upwards, move lure up and back, keeping it close to dog's muzzle. 9) "Good sit, Phoenix!"

10) *"Phoenix, stand!"* 11) *Move lure away from dog at nose height, then lower it a tad.* 12) *"Phoenix, off! Good stand, Phoenix!"* 13) *"Phoenix, down!"* 14) *Hand palm downwards, move lure down to lie between dog's forepaws.* 15) *"Phoenix, off! Good down-stay, Phoenix!"* 16) *"Phoenix, stand!"* 17) *Move lure away from dog's muzzle up to nose height.* 18) *"Phoenix, off! Good stand-stay, Phoenix. Now we'll make the vet and groomer happy!"*

as the dog stands, lower the lure to just beneath the dog's chin to entice him to look down; otherwise he will stand and then sit immediately. To prompt the dog to stand from the down position, move the lure half a dog-length upwards and away from the dog, holding the lure at standing nose height from the floor.

Teaching **rollover** is best started from the down position, with the dog lying on one side, or at least with both hind legs stretched out on the same side. Say "Fido, bang!" and move the lure backwards and alongside the dog's muzzle to its elbow (on the side of its outstretched hind legs). Once the dog looks to the side and backwards, very slowly move the lure upwards to the dog's shoulder and backbone. Tickling the dog in the goolies (groin area) often invokes a reflex-raising of the hind leg as an appeasement gesture, which facilitates the tendency to roll over. If you move the lure too quickly and the dog jumps into the standing position, have patience and start again. As soon as the dog rolls onto its back, keep the lure stationary and mesmerize the dog with a relaxing tummy rub.

To teach **rollover-stay** when the dog is standing or moving, say "Fido, bang!" and give the appropriate hand signal (with index finger pointed and thumb cocked in true Sam Spade fashion), then in one fluid movement lure him to first lie down and then rollover-stay as above.

Teaching the dog to *stay* in each of the above four positions becomes a piece of cake after first teaching the dog not to worry at the toy or treat training lure. This is best accomplished by hand feeding dinner kibble. Hold a piece of kibble firmly in your hand and softly instruct "Off!" Ignore any licking and slobbering *for however long the dog worries at the treat*, but say "Take it!" and offer the kibble *the instant* the dog breaks contact with his muzzle. Repeat this a few times, and then up the ante and insist the dog remove his muzzle for one whole second before offering the kibble. Then progressively refine your criteria and have the dog not touch your hand (or treat) for longer and longer periods on each trial, such as for two seconds, four seconds, then six, ten, fifteen, twenty, thirty seconds and so on. The dog soon learns: (1) worrying at the treat never gets results, whereas (2) noncontact is often rewarded after a variable time lapse.

Teaching *"Off!"* has many useful applications in its own right. Additionally, instructing the dog not to touch a training lure often produces spontaneous and magical stays. Request the dog to stand-stay, for example, and not to touch the lure. At first set your sights on a short two-second stay before rewarding the dog. (Remember, every long journey begins with a single step.) However, on subsequent trials, gradually and progressively increase the length of stay required to receive a reward. In no time at all your dog will stand calmly for a minute or so.

Relevancy Training

Once you have taught the dog what you expect her to do when requested to come, sit, lie down, stand, rollover and stay, the time is right to teach the dog *why* she should comply with your wishes. The secret is to have many (*many*) extremely short training interludes (two to five seconds each) at numerous (*numerous*) times during the course of the dog's day. Especially work with the dog immediately *before* the dog's good times and *during* the dog's good times. For example, ask your dog to sit and/or lie down each time before opening doors, serving meals, offering treats and tummy rubs; ask the dog to perform a few controlled doggy push-ups before letting her off-leash or throwing a tennis ball; and perhaps request the dog to sit-down-sit-stand-down-stand-rollover before inviting her to cuddle on the couch.

Similarly, request the dog to sit many times during play or on walks, and in no time at all the dog will be only too pleased to follow your instructions because he has learned that a compliant response heralds all sorts of goodies. Basically all you are trying to teach the dog is how to say please: "Please throw the tennis ball. Please may I snuggle on the couch."

Remember, whereas it is important to keep training interludes short, it is equally important to have many short sessions each and every day. The shortest (and most useful) session comprises asking the dog to sit and then go play during a play session. When trained this way, your dog will soon associate training with good times. In fact, the dog may be unable to distinguish between training and good times and, indeed, there should be no distinction. The warped concept that training involves forcing the dog to comply and/or dominating his will is totally at odds with the picture of a truly well-trained dog. In reality, enjoying a game of training with a dog is no different from enjoying a game of backgammon or tennis with a friend; and walking with a dog should be no different from strolling with buddies on the golf course.

Walk by Your Side

Many people attempt to teach a dog to heel by putting him on a leash and physically correcting the dog when he makes mistakes. There are a number of things seriously wrong with this approach, the first being that most people do not want precision heeling; rather, they simply want the dog to follow or walk by their side. Second, when physically restrained during "training," even though the dog may grudgingly mope by your side when "handcuffed" on leash, let's see what happens when he is off leash. History! The dog is in the next county because he never enjoyed walking with you on leash and you have no control over him off leash. So let's just teach the dog off leash from the outset to *want* to walk with us. Third, if the dog has not been trained to heel, it is a trifle hasty to think about punishing the poor dog for making mistakes and breaking heeling rules he didn't even know existed. This is simply not fair! Surely, if the dog had been adequately taught how to heel, he would seldom make mistakes and hence there would be no need to correct the dog. Remember, each mistake and each correction (punishment) advertise the trainer's inadequacy, not the dog's. The dog is not stubborn, he is not stupid and he is not bad. Even if he were, he would still require training, so let's train him properly.

Let's teach the dog to *enjoy* following us and to *want* to walk by our side offleash. Then it will be easier to teach high-precision off-leash heeling patterns if desired. After attaching the leash for safety on outdoor walks, but before going anywhere, it is necessary to teach the dog specifically not to pull. Now it will be much easier to teach on-leash walking and heeling because the dog already wants to walk with you, he is familiar with the desired walking and heeling positions and he knows not to pull.

FOLLOWING

Start by training your dog to follow you. Many puppies will follow if you simply walk away from them and maybe click your fingers or chuckle. Adult dogs may require additional enticement to stimulate them to follow, such as a training lure or, at the very least, a lively trainer. To teach the dog to follow: (1) keep walking and (2) walk away from the dog. If the dog attempts to lead or lag, change pace; slow down if the dog forges too far ahead, but speed up if he lags too far behind. Say "Steady!" or "Easy!" each time before you slow down and "Quickly!" or "Hustle!" each time before you speed up, and the dog will learn to change pace on cue. If the dog lags or leads too far, or if he wanders right or left, simply walk quickly in the opposite direction and maybe even run away from the dog and hide.

Practicing is a lot of fun; you can set up a course in your home, yard or park to do this. Indoors, entice the dog to follow upstairs, into a bedroom, into the bathroom, downstairs, around the living room couch, zigzagging between dining room chairs and into the kitchen for dinner. Outdoors, get the dog to follow around park benches, trees, shrubs and along walkways and lines in the grass. (For safety outdoors, it is advisable to attach a long line on the dog, but never exert corrective tension on the line.)

Remember, following has a lot to do with attitude—
your attitude! Most probably your dog will *not* want to
follow Mr. Grumpy Troll with the personality of wilted
lettuce. Lighten up—walk with a jaunty step, whistle a
happy tune, sing, skip and tell jokes to your dog and he
will be right there by your side.

BY YOUR SIDE

It is smart to train the dog to walk close on one side or
the other—either side will do, your choice. When walking, jogging or cycling, it is generally bad news to have
the dog suddenly cut in front of you. In fact, I train my
dogs to walk "By my side" and "Other side"—both very
useful instructions. It is possible to position the dog
fairly accurately by looking to the appropriate side and
clicking your fingers or slapping your thigh on that
side. A precise positioning may be attained by holding
a training lure, such as a chewtoy, tennis ball, or food
treat. Stop and stand still several times throughout the
walk, just as you would when window shopping or
meeting a friend. Use the lure to make sure the dog
slows down and stays close whenever you stop.

When teaching the dog to heel, we generally want
her to sit in heel position when we stop. Teach heel

*Using a toy to teach sit-heel-sit sequences: 1) "Phoenix, heel!" Standing still, move lure up and back
over dog's muzzle.... 2) To position dog sitting in heel position on your left side. 3) "Phoenix, heel!"
wagging lure in left hand. Change lure to right hand in preparation for sit signal.*

position at the standstill and the dog will learn that the default heel position is sitting by your side (left or right—your choice, unless you wish to compete in obedience trials, in which case the dog must heel on the left).

Several times a day, stand up and call your dog to come and sit in heel position—"Fido, heel!" For example, instruct the dog to come to heel each time there are commercials on TV, or each time you turn a page of a novel, and the dog will get it in a single evening.

Practice straight-line heeling and turns separately. With the dog sitting at heel, teach him to turn in place. After each quarter-turn, half-turn or full turn in place, lure the dog to sit at heel. Now it's time for short straight-line heeling sequences, no more than a few steps at a time. Always think of heeling in terms of Sit-Heel-Sit sequences—start and end with the dog in position and do your best to keep him there when moving. Progressively increase the number of steps in each sequence. When the dog remains close for 20 yards of straight-line heeling, it is time to add a few turns and then sign up for a happy-heeling obedience class to get some advice from the experts.

4) Use hand signal only to lure dog to sit as you stop. Eventually, dog will sit automatically at heel whenever you stop. 5) "Good dog!"

No Pulling on Leash

You can start teaching your dog not to pull on leash anywhere—in front of the television or outdoors—but regardless of location, you must not take a single step with tension in the leash. For a reason known only to dogs, even just a couple of paces of pulling on leash is intrinsically motivating and diabolically rewarding. Instead, attach the leash to the dog's collar, grasp the other end firmly with both hands held close to your chest, and stand still—do not budge an inch. Have somebody watch you with a stopwatch to time your progress, or else you will never believe this will work and so you will not even try the exercise, and your shoulder and the dog's neck will be traumatized for years to come.

Stand still and wait for the dog to stop pulling, and to sit and/or lie down. All dogs stop pulling and sit eventually. Most take only a couple of minutes; the all-time record is 22 ⅕ minutes. Time how long it takes. Gently praise the dog when he stops pulling, and as soon as he sits, enthusiastically praise the dog and take just one step forwards, then immediately stand still. This single step usually demonstrates the ballistic reinforcing nature of pulling on leash; most dogs explode to the end of the leash, so be prepared for the strain. Stand firm and wait for the dog to sit again. Repeat this half a dozen times and you will probably notice a progressive reduction in the force of the dog's one-step explosions and a radical reduction in the time it takes for the dog to sit each time.

As the dog learns "Sit we go" and "Pull we stop," she will begin to walk forward calmly with each single step and automatically sit when you stop. Now try two steps before you stop. Wooooooo! Scary! When the dog has mastered two steps at a time, try for three. After each success, progressively increase the number of steps in the sequence: try four steps and then six, eight, ten and twenty steps before stopping. Congratulations! You are now walking the dog on leash.

Whenever walking with the dog (off leash or on leash), make sure you stop periodically to practice a few position commands and stays before instructing the dog to "Walk on!" (Remember, you want the dog to be compliant everywhere, not just in the kitchen when his dinner is at hand.) For example, stopping every 25 yards to briefly train the dog amounts to over 200 training interludes within a single three-mile stroll. And each training session is in a different location. You will not believe the improvement within just the first mile of the first walk.

To put it another way, integrating training into a walk offers 200 separate opportunities to use the continuance of the walk as a reward to reinforce the dog's education. Moreover, some training interludes may comprise continuing education for the dog's walking skills: Alternate short periods of the dog walking calmly by your side with periods when the dog is allowed to sniff and investigate the environment. Now sniffing odors on the grass and meeting other dogs become rewards which reinforce the dog's calm and mannerly demeanor. Good Lord! Whatever next? Many enjoyable walks together of course. Happy trails!

Enjoying
Your
Dog

THE IMPORTANCE OF TRICKS

Nothing will improve a dog's quality of life better than having a few tricks under its belt. Teaching any trick expands the dog's vocabulary, which facilitates communication and improves the owner's control. Also, specific tricks help prevent and resolve specific behavior problems. For example, by teaching the dog to fetch his toys, the dog learns carrying a toy makes the owner happy and, therefore, will be more likely to chew his toy than other inappropriate items.

More important, teaching tricks prompts owners to lighten up and train with a sunny disposition. Really, tricks should be no different from any other behaviors we put on cue. But they are. When teaching tricks, owners have a much sweeter attitude, which in turn motivates the dog and improves her willingness to comply. The dog feels tricks are a blast, but formal commands are a drag. In fact, tricks are so enjoyable, they may be used as rewards in training by asking the dog to come, sit and down-stay and then rollover for a tummy rub. Go on, try it: Crack a smile and even giggle when the dog promptly and willingly lies down and stays.

Most important, performing tricks prompts onlookers to smile and giggle. Many people are scared of dogs, especially large ones. And nothing can be more off-putting for a dog than to be constantly confronted by strangers who don't like him because of his size or the way he looks. Uneasy people put the dog on edge, causing him to back off and bark, only frightening people all the more. And so a vicious circle develops, with the people's fear fueling the dog's fear *and vice versa*. Instead, tie a pink ribbon to your dog's collar and practice all sorts of tricks on walks and in the park, and you will be pleasantly amazed how it changes people's attitudes toward your friendly dog. The dog's repertoire of tricks is limited only by the trainer's imagination. Below I have described three of my favorites:

SPEAK AND SHUSH

The training sequence involved in teaching a dog to bark on request is no different from that used when training any behavior on cue: request—lure—response—reward. As always, the secret of success lies in finding an effective lure. If the dog always barks at the doorbell, for example, say "Rover, speak!", have an accomplice ring the doorbell, then reward the dog for barking. After a few woofs, ask Rover to "Shush!", waggle a food treat under his nose (to entice him to sniff and thus to shush), praise him when quiet and eventually offer the treat as a reward. Alternate "Speak" and "Shush," progressively increasing the length of shush-time between each barking bout.

PLAYBOW

With the dog standing, say "Bow!" and lower the food lure (palm upwards) to rest between the dog's forepaws. Praise as the dog lowers

126

her forequarters and sternum to the ground (as when teaching the down), but then lure the dog to stand and offer the treat. On successive trials, gradually increase the length of time the dog is required to remain in the playbow posture in order to gain a food reward. If the dog's rear end collapses into a down, say nothing and offer no reward; simply start over.

BE A BEAR

With the dog sitting backed into a corner to prevent him from toppling over backwards, say "Be a Bear!" With bent paw and palm down, raise a lure upwards and backwards along the top of the dog's muzzle. Praise the dog when he sits up on his haunches and offer the treat as a reward. To prevent the dog from standing on his hind legs, keep the lure closer to the dog's muzzle. On each trial, progressively increase the length of time the dog is required to sit up to receive a food reward. Since lure/reward training is so easy, teach the dog to stand and walk on his hind legs as well!

Teaching "Be a Bear"

chapter 9

Getting
Active
with your Dog

by Bardi McLennan

Once you and your dog have graduated from basic obedience training and are beginning to work together as a team, you can take part in the growing world of dog activities. There are so many fun things to do with your dog! Just remember, people and dogs don't always learn at the same pace, so don't be upset if you (or your dog) need more than two basic training courses before your team becomes operational. Even smart dogs don't go straight to college from kindergarten!

Just as there are events geared to certain types of dogs, so there are ones that are more appealing to certain types of people. In some activities, you give the commands and your dog does the work (upland game hunting is one example), while in others, such as agility, you'll both get a workout. You may want to aim for prestigious titles to add to your dog's name, or you may want nothing more than the sheer enjoyment of being around other people and their dogs. Passive or active, participation has its own rewards.

Consider your dog's physical capabilities when looking into any of the canine activities. It's easy to see that a Basset Hound is not built for the racetrack, nor would a Chihuahua be the breed of choice for pulling a sled. A loyal dog will attempt almost anything you ask him to do, so it is up to you to know your

All dogs seem to love playing flyball.

dog's limitations. A dog must be physically sound in order to compete at any level in athletic activities, and being mentally sound is a definite plus. Advanced age, however, may not be a deterrent. Many dogs still hunt and herd at ten or twelve years of age. It's entirely possible for dogs to be "fit at 50." Take your dog for a checkup, explain to your vet the type of activity you have in mind and be guided by his or her findings.

You needn't be restricted to breed-specific sports if it's only fun you're after. Certain AKC activities are limited to designated breeds; however, as each new trial, test or sport has grown in popularity, so has the variety of breeds encouraged to participate at a fun level.

But don't shortchange your fun, or that of your dog, by thinking only of the basic function of her breed. Once a dog has learned how to learn, she can be taught to do just about anything as long as the size of the dog is right for the job and you both think it is fun and rewarding. In other words, you are a team.

To get involved in any of the activities detailed in this chapter, look for the names and addresses of the organizations that sponsor them in Chapter 13. You can also ask your breeder or a local dog trainer for contacts.

You can compete in obedience trials with a well trained dog.

Official American Kennel Club Activities

The following tests and trials are some of the events sanctioned by the AKC and sponsored by various dog clubs. Your dog's expertise will be rewarded with impressive titles. You can participate just for fun, or be competitive and go for those awards.

OBEDIENCE

Training classes begin with pups as young as three months of age in kindergarten puppy training, then advance to pre-novice (all exercises on lead) and go on to novice, which is where you'll start off-lead work. In obedience classes dogs learn to sit, stay, heel and come through a variety of exercises. Once you've got the basics down, you can enter obedience trials and work toward earning your dog's first degree, a C.D. (Companion Dog).

The next level is called "Open," in which jumps and retrieves perk up the dog's interest. Passing grades in competition at this level earn a C.D.X. (Companion Dog Excellent). Beyond that lies the goal of the most ambitious—Utility (U.D. and even U.D.X. or OTCh, an Obedience Champion).

AGILITY

All dogs can participate in the latest canine sport to have gained worldwide popularity for its fun and excitement, agility. It began in England as a canine version of horse show-jumping, but because dogs are more agile and able to perform on verbal commands, extra feats were added such as climbing, balancing and racing through tunnels or in and out of weave poles.

Many of the obstacles (regulation or homemade) can be set up in your own backyard. If the agility bug bites, you could end up in international competition!

For starters, your dog should be obedience trained, even though, in the beginning, the lessons may all be taught on lead. Once the dog understands the commands (and you do, too), it's as easy as guiding the dog over a prescribed course, one obstacle at a time. In competition, the race is against the clock, so wear your running shoes! The dog starts with 200 points and the judge deducts for infractions and misadventures along the way.

All dogs seem to love agility and respond to it as if they were being turned loose in a playground paradise. Your dog's enthusiasm will be contagious; agility turns into great fun for dog and owner.

FIELD TRIALS AND HUNTING TESTS

There are field trials and hunting tests for the sporting breeds—retrievers, spaniels and pointing breeds, and for some hounds—Bassets, Beagles and Dachshunds. Field trials are competitive events that test a dog's ability to perform the functions for which she was bred. Hunting tests, which are open to retrievers,

---

TITLES AWARDED BY THE AKC

Conformation: Ch. (Champion)

Obedience: CD (Companion Dog); CDX (Companion Dog Excellent); UD (Utility Dog); UDX (Utility Dog Excellent); OTCh. (Obedience Trial Champion)

Field: JH (Junior Hunter); SH (Senior Hunter); MH (Master Hunter); AFCh. (Amateur Field Champion); FCh. (Field Champion)

Lure Coursing: JC (Junior Courser); SC (Senior Courser)

Herding: HT (Herding Tested); PT (Pre-Trial Tested); HS (Herding Started); HI (Herding Intermediate); HX (Herding Excellent); HCh. (Herding Champion)

Tracking: TD (Tracking Dog); TDX (Tracking Dog Excellent)

Agility: NAD (Novice Agility); OAD (Open Agility); ADX (Agility Excellent); MAX (Master Agility)

Earthdog Tests: JE (Junior Earthdog); SE (Senior Earthdog); ME (Master Earthdog)

Canine Good Citizen: CGC

Combination: DC (Dual Champion—Ch. and Fch.); TC (Triple Champion—Ch., Fch., and OTCh.)

spaniels and pointing breeds only, are noncompetitive and are a means of judging the dog's ability as well as that of the handler.

Hunting is a very large and complex part of canine sports, and if you own one of the breeds that hunts, the events are a great treat for your dog and you. He gets to do what he was bred for, and you get to work with him and watch him do it. You'll be proud of and amazed at what your dog can do.

Fortunately, the AKC publishes a series of booklets on these events, which outline the rules and regulations and include a glossary of the sometimes complicated terms. The AKC also publishes newsletters for field trialers and hunting test enthusiasts. The United Kennel Club (UKC) also has informative materials for the hunter and his dog.

Retrievers and other sporting breeds get to do what they're bred to in hunting tests.

HERDING TESTS AND TRIALS

Herding, like hunting, dates back to the first known uses man made of dogs. The interest in herding today is widespread, and if you own a herding breed, you can join in the activity. Herding dogs are tested for their natural skills to keep a flock of ducks, sheep or cattle together. If your dog shows potential, you can start at the testing level, where your dog can earn a title for showing an inherent herding ability. With training you can advance to the trial level, where your dog should be capable of controlling even difficult livestock in diverse situations.

LURE COURSING

The AKC Tests and Trials for Lure Coursing are open to traditional sighthounds—Greyhounds, Whippets,

Borzoi, Salukis, Afghan Hounds, Ibizan Hounds and Scottish Deerhounds—as well as to Basenjis and Rhodesian Ridgebacks. Hounds are judged on overall ability, follow, speed, agility and endurance. This is possibly the most exciting of the trials for spectators, because the speed and agility of the dogs is awesome to watch as they chase the lure (or "course") in heats of two or three dogs at a time.

TRACKING

Tracking is another activity in which almost any dog can compete because every dog that sniffs the ground when taken outdoors is, in fact, tracking. The hard part comes when the rules as to what, when and where the dog tracks are determined by a person, not the dog! Tracking tests cover a large area of fields, woods and roads. The tracks are laid hours before the dogs go to work on them, and include "tricks" like cross-tracks and sharp turns. If you're interested in search-and-rescue work, this is the place to start.

This tracking dog is hot on the trail.

EARTHDOG TESTS FOR SMALL TERRIERS AND DACHSHUNDS

These tests are open to Australian, Bedlington, Border, Cairn, Dandie Dinmont, Smooth and Wire Fox, Lakeland, Norfolk, Norwich, Scottish, Sealyham, Skye, Welsh and West Highland White Terriers as well as Dachshunds. The dogs need no prior training for this terrier sport. There is a qualifying test on the day of the event, so dog and handler learn the rules on the spot. These tests, or "digs," sometimes end with informal races in the late afternoon.

Here are some of the extracurricular obedience and racing activities that are not regulated by the AKC or UKC, but are generally run by clubs or a group of dog fanciers and are often open to all.

Canine Freestyle This activity is something new on the scene and is variously likened to dancing, dressage or ice skating. It is meant to show the athleticism of the dog, but also requires showmanship on the part of the dog's handler. If you and your dog like to ham it up for friends, you might want to look into freestyle.

Lure coursing lets sighthounds do what they do best—run!

Scent Hurdle Racing Scent hurdle racing is purely a fun activity sponsored by obedience clubs with members forming competing teams. The height of the hurdles is based on the size of the shortest dog on the team. On a signal, one team dog is released on each of two side-by-side courses and must clear every hurdle before picking up its own dumbbell from a platform and returning over the jumps to the handler. As each dog returns, the next on that team is sent. Of course, that is what the dogs are supposed to do. When the dogs improvise (going under or around the hurdles, stealing another dog's dumbbell, and so forth), it no doubt frustrates the handlers, but just adds to the fun for everyone else.

Flyball This type of racing is similar, but after negotiating the four hurdles, the dog comes to a flyball box, steps on a lever that releases a tennis ball into the air, catches the ball and returns over the hurdles to the starting point. This game also becomes extremely fun for spectators because the dogs sometimes cheat by catching a ball released by the dog in the next lane. Three titles can be earned—Flyball Dog (F.D.), Flyball Dog Excellent (F.D.X.) and Flyball Dog Champion (Fb.D.Ch.)—all awarded by the North American Flyball Association, Inc.

Dogsledding The name conjures up the Rocky Mountains or the frigid North, but you can find dogsled clubs in such unlikely spots as Maryland, North Carolina and Virginia! Dogsledding is primarily for the Nordic breeds such as the Alaskan Malamutes, Siberian Huskies and Samoyeds, but other breeds can try. There are some practical backyard applications to this sport, too. With parental supervision, almost any strong dog could pull a child's sled.

Coming over the A-frame on an agility course.

These are just some of the many recreational ways you can get to know and understand your multifaceted dog better and have fun doing it.

chapter 10

Your Dog
and your
Family

by Bardi McLennan

Adding a dog automatically increases your family by one, no matter whether you live alone in an apartment or are part of a mother, father and six kids household. The single-person family is fair game for numerous and varied canine misconceptions as to who is dog and who pays the bills, whereas a dog in a houseful of children will consider himself to be just one of the gang, littermates all. One dog and one child may give a dog reason to believe they are both kids or both dogs.

Either interpretation requires parental supervision and sometimes speedy intervention.

As soon as one paw goes through the door into your home, Rufus (or Rufina) has to make many adjustments to become a part of your family. Your job is to make him fit in as painlessly as possible. An older dog may have some frame of reference from past experience, but to a 10-week-old puppy, everything is brand new: people, furniture, stairs, when and where people eat, sleep or watch TV, his own place and everyone else's space, smells, sounds, outdoors—everything!

Puppies, and newly acquired dogs of any age, do not need what we think of as "freedom." If you leave a new dog or puppy loose in the house, you will almost certainly return to chaotic destruction and the dog will forever after equate your homecoming with a time of punishment to be dreaded. It is unfair to give your dog what amounts to "freedom to get into trouble." Instead, confine him to a crate for brief periods of your absence (up to three or four hours) and, for the long haul, a workday for example, confine him to one untrashable area with his own toys, a bowl of water and a radio left on (low) in another room.

Lots of pets get along with each other just fine.

For the first few days, when not confined, put Rufus on a long leash tied to your wrist or waist. This umbilical cord method enables the dog to learn all about you from your body language and voice, and to learn by his own actions which things in the house are NO! and which ones are rewarded by "Good dog." House-training will be easier with the pup always by your side. Speaking of which, accidents do happen. That goal of "completely housetrained" takes up to a year, or the length of time it takes the pup to mature.

The All-Adult Family

Most dogs in an adults-only household today are likely to be latchkey pets, with no one home all day but the dog. When you return after a tough day on the job, the dog can and should be your relaxation therapy. But going home can instead be a daily frustration.

Separation anxiety is a very common problem for the dog in a working household. It may begin with whines and barks of loneliness, but it will soon escalate into a frenzied destruction derby. That is why it is so important to set aside the time to teach a dog to relax when left alone in his confined area and to understand that he can trust you to return.

Let the dog get used to your work schedule in easy stages. Confine him to one room and go in and out of that room over and over again. Be casual about it. No physical, voice or eye contact. When the pup no longer even notices your comings and goings, leave the house for varying lengths of time, returning to stay home for a few minutes and gradually increasing the time away. This training can take days, but the dog is learning that you haven't left him forever and that he can trust you.

Any time you leave the dog, but especially during this training period, be casual about your departure. No anxiety-building fond farewells. Just "Bye" and go! Remember the "Good dog" when you return to find everything more or less as you left it.

If things are a mess (or even a disaster) when you return, greet the dog, take him outside to eliminate, and then put him in his crate while you clean up. Rant and rave in the shower! *Do not* punish the dog. You were not there when it happened, and the rule is: Only punish as you catch the dog in the act of wrongdoing. Obviously, it makes sense to get your latchkey puppy when you'll have a week or two to spend on these training essentials.

Family weekend activities should include Rufus whenever possible. Depending on the pup's age, now is the time for a long walk in the park, playtime in the backyard, a hike in the woods. Socializing is as important as health care, good food and physical exercise, so visiting Aunt Emma or Uncle Harry and the next-door neighbor's dog or cat is essential to developing an outgoing, friendly temperament in your pet.

If you are a single adult, socializing Rufus at home and away will prevent him from becoming overly protective of you (or just overly attached) and will also prevent such behavioral problems as dominance or fear of strangers.

Babies

Whether already here or on the way, babies figure larger than life in the eyes of a dog. If the dog is there first, let him in on all your baby preparations in the house. When baby arrives, let Rufus sniff any item of clothing that has been on the baby before Junior comes home. Then let Mom greet the dog first before introducing the new family member. Hold the baby down for the dog to see and sniff, but make sure some-

one's holding the dog on lead in case of any sudden moves. Don't play keep-away or tease the dog with the baby, which only invites undesirable jumping up.

The dog and the baby are "family," and for starters, can be treated almost as equals. Things rapidly change, however, especially when baby takes to creeping around on all fours on the dog's turf or, better yet, has yummy pudding all over her face and hands! That's when a lot of things in the dog's and baby's lives become more separate than equal.

Dogs are perfect confidants.

Toddlers make terrible dog owners, but if you can't avoid the combination, use patient discipline (that is, positive teaching rather than punishment), and use time-outs before you run out of patience.

139

A dog and a baby (or toddler, or an assertive young child) should never be left alone together. Take the dog with you or confine him. With a baby or youngsters in the house, you'll have plenty of use for that wonderful canine safety device called a crate!

Young Children

Any dog in a house with kids will behave pretty much as the kids do, good or bad. But even good dogs and good children can get into trouble when play becomes rowdy and active.

Teach children how to play nicely with a puppy.

Legs bobbing up and down, shrill voices screeching, a ball hurtling overhead, all add up to exuberant frustration for a dog who's just trying to be part of the gang. In a pack of puppies, any legs or toys being chased would be caught by a set of teeth, and all the pups involved would understand that is how the game is played. Kids do not understand this, nor do parents tolerate it. Bring Rufus indoors before you have reason to regret it. This is time-out, not a punishment.

You can explain the situation to the children and tell them they must play quieter games until the puppy learns not to grab them with his mouth. Unfortunately, you can't explain it that easily to the dog. With adult supervision, they will learn how to play together.

Young children love to tease. Sticking their faces or wiggling their hands or fingers in the dog's face is teasing. To another person it might be just annoying, but it is threatening to a dog. There's another difference: We can make the child stop by an explanation, but the only way a dog can stop it is with a warning growl and then with teeth. Teasing is the major cause of children being bitten by their pets. Treat it seriously.

Older Children

The best age for a child to get a first dog is between the ages of 8 and 12. That's when kids are able to accept some real responsibility for their pet. Even so, take the child's vow of "I will never *ever* forget to feed (brush, walk, etc.) the dog" for what it's worth: a child's good intention at that moment. Most kids today have extra lessons, soccer practice, Little League, ballet, and so forth piled on top of school schedules. There will be many times when Mom will have to come to the dog's rescue. "I walked the dog for you so you can set the table for me" is one way to get around a missed appointment without laying on blame or guilt.

Kids in this age group make excellent obedience trainers because they are into the teaching/learning process themselves and they lack the self-consciousness of adults. Attending a dog show is something the whole family can enjoy, and watching Junior Showmanship may catch the eye of the kids. Older children can begin to get involved in many of the recreational activities that were reviewed in the previous chapter. Some of the agility obstacles, for example, can be set up in the backyard as a family project (with an adult making sure all the equipment is safe and secure for the dog).

Older kids are also beginning to look to the future, and may envision themselves as veterinarians or trainers or show dog handlers or writers of the next Lassie best-seller. Dogs are perfect confidants for these dreams. They won't tell a soul.

Other Pets

Introduce all pets tactfully. In a dog/cat situation, hold the dog, not the cat. Let two dogs meet on neutral turf—a stroll in the park or a walk down the street—with both on loose leads to permit all the normal canine ways of saying hello, including routine sniffing, circling, more sniffing, and so on. Small creatures such as hamsters, chinchillas or mice must be kept safe from their natural predators (dogs and cats).

Festive Family Occasions

Parties are great for people, but not necessarily for puppies. Until all the guests have arrived, put the dog in his crate or in a room where he won't be disturbed. A socialized dog can join the fun later as long as he's not underfoot, annoying guests or into the hors d'oeuvres.

There are a few dangers to consider, too. Doors opening and closing can allow a puppy to slip out unnoticed in the confusion, and you'll be organizing a search party instead of playing host or hostess. Party food and buffet service are not for dogs. Let Rufus party in his crate with a nice big dog biscuit.

At Christmas time, not only are tree decorations dangerous and breakable (and perhaps family heirlooms), but extreme caution should be taken with the lights, cords and outlets for the tree lights and any other festive lighting. Occasionally a dog lifts a leg, ignoring the fact that the tree is indoors. To avoid this, use a canine repellent, made for gardens, on the tree. Or keep him out of the tree room unless supervised. And whatever you do, *don't* invite trouble by hanging his toys on the tree!

Car Travel

Before you plan a vacation by car or RV with Rufus, be sure he enjoys car travel. Nothing spoils a holiday quicker than a carsick dog! Work within the dog's comfort level. Get in the car with the dog in his crate or attached to a canine car safety belt and just sit there until he relaxes. That's all. Next time, get in the car, turn on the engine and go nowhere. Just sit. When that is okay, turn on the engine and go around the block. Now you can go for a ride and include a stop where you get out, leaving the dog for a minute or two.

On a warm day, always park in the shade and leave windows open several inches. And return quickly. It only takes 10 minutes for a car to become an overheated steel death trap.

Motel or Pet Motel?

Not all motels or hotels accept pets, but you have a much better choice today than even a few years ago. To find a dog-friendly lodging, look at *On the Road Again With Man's Best Friend*, a series of directories that detail bed and breakfasts, inns, family resorts and other hotels/motels. Some places require a refundable deposit to cover any damage incurred by the dog. More B&Bs accept pets now, but some restrict the size.

If taking Rufus with you is not feasible, check out boarding kennels in your area. Your veterinarian may offer this service, or recommend a kennel or two he or she is familiar with. Go see the facilities for yourself, ask about exercise, diet, housing, and so on. Or, if you'd rather have Rufus stay home, look into bonded petsitters, many of whom will also bring in the mail and water your plants.

chapter 11

Your Dog
and your
Community

by Bardi McLennan

Step outside your home with your dog and you are no longer just family, you are both part of your community. This is when the phrase "responsible pet ownership" takes on serious implications. For starters, it means you pick up after your dog—not just occasionally, but every time your dog eliminates away from home. That means you have joined the Plastic Baggy Brigade! You always have plastic sandwich bags in your pocket and several in the car. It means you teach your kids how to use them, too. If you think this is "yucky," just imagine what

the person (a non-doggy person) who inadvertently steps in the mess thinks!

Your responsibility extends to your neighbors: To their ears (no annoying barking); to their property (their garbage, their lawn, their flower beds, their cat—especially their cat); to their kids (on bikes, at play); to their kids' toys and sports equipment.

There are numerous dog-related laws, ranging from simple dog licensing and leash laws to those holding you liable for any physical injury or property damage done by your dog. These laws are in place to protect everyone in the community, including you and your dog. There are town ordinances and state laws which are by no means the same in all towns or all states. Ignorance of the law won't get you off the hook. The time to find out what the laws are where you live is now.

Be sure your dog's license is current. This is not just a good local ordinance, it can make the difference between finding your lost dog or not.

Dressing your dog up makes him appealing to strangers.

Many states now require proof of rabies vaccination and that the dog has been spayed or neutered before issuing a license. At the same time, keep up the dog's annual immunizations.

Never let your dog run loose in the neighborhood. This will not only keep you on the right side of the leash law, it's the outdoor version of the rule about not giving your dog "freedom to get into trouble."

Good Canine Citizen

Sometimes it's hard for a dog's owner to assess whether or not the dog is sufficiently socialized to be accepted by the community at large. Does Rufus or Rufina display good, controlled behavior in public? The AKC's Canine Good Citizen program is available through many dog organizations. If your dog passes the test, the title "CGC" is earned.

The overall purpose is to turn your dog into a good neighbor and to teach you about your responsibility to your community as a dog owner. Here are the ten things your dog must do willingly:

1. Allow a stranger to handle him or her as a groomer or veterinarian would.
2. Accept a stranger stopping to chat with you.
3. Walk nicely on a loose lead.
4. Walk calmly through a crowd.
5. Sit and be petted by a stranger.
6. Sit and down on command.
7. Stay put when you move away.
8. Casually greet another dog.
9. React confidently to distractions.
10. Accept being tied up in a strange place and left alone for a few minutes.

Schools and Dogs

Schools are getting involved with pet ownership on an educational level. It has been proven that children who are kind to animals are humane in their attitude toward other people as adults.

A dog is a child's best friend, and so children are often primary pet owners, if not the primary caregivers. Unfortunately, they are also the ones most often bitten by dogs. This occurs due to a lack of understanding that pets, no matter how sweet, cuddly and loving, are still animals. Schools, along with parents, dog clubs, dog fanciers and the AKC, are working to change all that with video programs for children not only in grade school, but in the nursery school and pre-kindergarten age group. Teaching youngsters how to be responsible dog owners is important community work. When your dog has a CGC, volunteer to take part in an educational classroom event put on by your dog club.

Boy Scout Merit Badge

A Merit Badge for Dog Care can be earned by any Boy Scout ages 11 to 18. The requirements are not easy, but amount to a complete course in responsible dog care and general ownership. Here are just a few of the things a Scout must do to earn that badge:

Point out ten parts of the dog using the correct names.

Give a report (signed by parent or guardian) on your care of the dog (feeding, food used, housing, exercising, grooming and bathing), plus what has been done to keep the dog healthy.

Explain the right way to obedience train a dog, and demonstrate three comments.

Several of the requirements have to do with health care, including first aid, handling a hurt dog, and the dangers of home treatment for a serious ailment.

The final requirement is to know the local laws and ordinances involving dogs.

There are similar programs for Girl Scouts and 4-H members.

Local Clubs

Local dog clubs are no longer in existence just to put on a yearly dog show. Today, they are apt to be the hub of the community's involvement with pets. Dog clubs conduct educational forums with big-name speakers, stage demonstrations of canine talent in a busy mall and take dogs of various breeds to schools for class-room discussion.

The quickest way to feel accepted as a member in a club is to volunteer your services! Offer to help with something—anything—and watch your popularity (and your interest) grow.

Therapy Dogs

Once your dog has earned that essential CGC and reliably demonstrates a steady, calm temperament, you could look into what therapy dogs are doing in your area.

Therapy dogs go with their owners to visit patients at hospitals or nursing homes, generally remaining on leash but able to coax a pat from a stiffened hand, a smile from a blank face, a few words from sealed lips or a hug from someone in need of love.

Your dog can make a difference in lots of lives.

Nursing homes cover a wide range of patient care. Some specialize in care of the elderly, some in the treatment of specific illnesses, some in physical therapy. Children's facilities also welcome visits from trained therapy dogs for boosting morale in their pediatric patients. Hospice care for the terminally ill and the at-home care of AIDS patients are other areas where this canine visiting is desperately needed. Therapy dog training comes first.

There is a lot more involved than just taking your nice friendly pooch to someone's bedside. Doing therapy dog work involves your own emotional stability as well as that of your dog. But once you have met all the requirements for this work, making the rounds once a week or once a month with your therapy dog is possibly the most rewarding of all community activities.

Disaster Aid

This community service is definitely not for everyone, partly because it is time-consuming. The initial training is rigorous, and there can be no let-up in the continuing workouts, because members are on call 24 hours a day to go wherever they are needed at a moment's notice. But if you think you would like to be able to assist in a disaster, look into search-and-rescue work. The network of search-and-rescue volunteers is worldwide, and all members of the American Rescue Dog Association (ARDA) who are qualified to do this work are volunteers who train and maintain their own dogs.

Physical Aid

Most people are familiar with Seeing Eye dogs, which serve as blind people's eyes, but not with all the other work that dogs are trained to do to assist the disabled. Dogs are also specially trained to pull wheelchairs, carry school books, pick up dropped objects, open and close doors. Some also are ears for the deaf. All these assistance-trained dogs, by the way, are allowed anywhere "No Pet" signs exist (as are therapy dogs when

properly identified). Getting started in any of this fascinating work requires a background in dog training and canine behavior, but there are also volunteer jobs ranging from answering the phone to cleaning out kennels to providing a foster home for a puppy. You have only to ask.

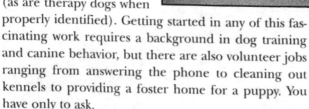

Making the rounds with your therapy dog can be very rewarding.

part four

Beyond
the

Basics

chapter 12

Recommended Reading

Books

GENERAL

American Kennel Club (AKC). *American Kennel Club Dog Care and Training.* New York: Howell Book House, 1991.

————. *The Complete Dog Book,* 19th Edition Revised. New York: Howell Book House, 1998.

Bamberger, Michelle, DVM. *Help! The Quick Guide to First Aid for Your Dog.* New York: Howell Book House, 1995.

Carlson, Liisa, DVM, and James Giffin, MD. *Dog Owners Home Veterinary Handbook,* 3rd Edition. New York: Howell Book House, 1999.

DeBitetto, James, DVM, and Sarah Hodgson. *You & Your Puppy.* New York: Howell Book House, 2000.

Rogers Clark, Anne, and Andrew H. Brace. *The International Encyclopedia of Dogs.* New York: Howell Book House, 1995.

Vella, Bob, and Ken Leebow. *300 Incredible Things for Pet Lovers on the Internet.* Marietta, Georgia: 300 Incredible.com, 2000.

Volhard, Wendy, and Kerry Brown, DVM. *Holistic Guide for a Healthy Dog.* New York: Howell Book House, 2000.

ABOUT DOG SHOWS

Alston, George. *The Winning Edge.* New York: Howell Book House, 1992.

Hall, Lynn. *Dog Showing for Beginners.* New York: Howell Book House, 1994.

ABOUT TRAINING

Arden, Andrea. *Dog-Friendly Dog Training*. New York: Howell Book House, 1999.

Benjamin, Carol Lea. *Dog Training for Kids*. New York: Howell Book House, 1988.

————. *Dog Training in 10 Minutes*. New York: Howell Book House, 1997.

Burch, Mary, PhD, and Jon Bailey. *How Dogs Learn*. New York: Howell Book House, 1999.

Dunbar, Ian, PhD, MRCVS. *Dog Behavior: An Owner's Guide to a Happy Healthy Pet*. New York: Howell Book House, 1996.

————. *How to Teach a New Dog Old Tricks*. James & Kenneth Publishers, 1998. Order from the publisher at 2140 Shattuck Ave. #2406, Berkeley, CA 94704. (510) 658-8588.

Evans, Job Michael. *People, Pooches and Problems*. New York: Howell Book House, 2001.

Hodgson, Sarah. *Dogperfect: The User Friendly Guide to a Well Behaved Dog*. New York: Howell Book House, 1995.

New Skete Monks. *How to Be Your Dog's Best Friend*. Boston: Little Brown & Company, 1978.

Pryor, Karen. *Don't Shoot the Dog! The New Art of Teaching and Training*, Revised Edition. New York: Bantam Doubleday Dell, 1999.

Rutherford, Clarice, and David H. Neil, MRCVS. *How to Raise a Puppy You Can Live With*. Loveland, Colorado: Alpine Publications, 1982.

Volhard, Jack, and Melissa Bartlett. *What All Good Dogs Should Know: The Sensible Way to Train*. New York: Howell Book House, 1991.

ABOUT BREEDING

Finder Harris, Beth J. *Breeding a Litter: The Complete Book of Prenatal and Postnatal Care*. New York: Howell Book House, 1993.

Holst, Phyllis. *Canine Reproduction: The Breeder's Guide*. Loveland, Colorado: Alpine Publications, 1999.

Walkowicz, Chris, and Bonnie Wilcox, DVM. *Successful Dog Breeding: The Complete Handbook of Canine Midwifery*. New York: Howell Book House, 1994.

American Rescue Dog Association. *Search and Rescue Dogs.* New York: Howell Book House, 1991.

Barwig, Susan, and Stewart Hilliard. *Schutzhund.* New York: Howell Book House, 1991.

Burch, Mary. *Volunteering with Your Pet.* New York: Howell Book House, 1996.

O'Neil, Jacqueline F. *All About Agility.* New York: Howell Book House, 1999.

Vollhard, Jack and Wendy. *The Canine Good Citizen.* New York: Howell Book House, 1994.

Magazines

The AKC GAZETTE, The Official Journal for the Sport of Purebred Dogs
American Kennel Club
260 Madison Avenue
New York, NY 10016
(212) 696-8200
www.akc.org

The Bark
2810 8th Street
Berkeley, CA 94710
(510) 704-0827
www.thebark.com

Dog Fancy
Fancy Publications
3 Burroughs
Irvine, CA 92718
(949) 855-8822
www.animalnetwork.com

Dog & Kennel
Pet Publishing, Inc.
7-L Dundas Circle
Greensboro, NC 27407
(336) 292-4047
www.dogandkennel.com

Dog Watch Newsletter
P.O. Box 420235
Palm Coast, FL 32142-0235
(800) 829-5574
www.vet.cornell.edu/publicresources/dog

Dog World
Primedia
500 North Dearborn, Suite 1100
Chicago, IL 60610
(877) 224-7711
www.dogworldmag.com

Videos

"SIRIUS Puppy Training," by Ian Dunbar, PhD, MRCVS.
James & Kenneth Publishers, 2140 Shattuck Ave. #2406,
Berkeley, CA 94704. Order from the publisher.

"Training the Companion Dog," from Dr. Dunbar's British
TV Series, James & Kenneth Publishers. (See address
above.)

The American Kennel Club produces videos on every
breed of dog, as well as on hunting tests, field trials and
other areas of interest to purebred dog owners. For more
information, write to AKC/Video Fulfillment, 5580
Centerview Dr., Suite 200, Raleigh, NC 27606. The AKC
can be reached at (919) 233-9767, or visit its Web site at
www.akc.org.

chapter 13

Resources

Breed Clubs and Registries

Registry organizations register purebred dogs. The American Kennel Club is the oldest and largest in the United States, and currently recognizes over 130 breeds. The United Kennel Club registers some breeds the AKC doesn't (including the American Pit Bull Terrier and the Miniature Fox Terrier), as well as many of the same breeds. The other clubs included here are for your reference; the AKC can provide you with a list of foreign registries.

Every breed recognized by the American Kennel Club has a national (parent) club. National clubs are a great source of information on your breed. You can get the name of the secretary of the club by contacting:

American Kennel Club (AKC)
260 Madison Avenue, 4th Floor
New York, NY 10016
(212) 696-8200
www.akc.org

For breeder referrals, call the customer service department in North Carolina at (919) 233-9767, or visit their Web site.

United Kennel Club (UKC)
100 East Kilgore Road
Portage, MI 49002-5584
(616) 343-9020
www.ukcdogs.com

American Rare Breed Association (ARBA)
9921 Frank Tippet Road
Cheltenham, MD 20612
(301) 868-5718
www.arba.org

Canadian Kennel Club (CKC)
89 Skyway Avenue
Etobicoke, Ontario
Canada M9W 6R4
(800) 250-8040
(416) 675-5511
information@ckc.ca

Health Registries

CERF
Department of Veterinary Clinical Science
School of Veterinary Medicine
Purdue University
West Lafayette, IN 47907
(765) 494-8179
yshen@vet.purdue.edu

Orthopedic Foundation for Animals (OFA)
2300 East Nifong Boulevard
Columbia, MO 65201-3856
(573) 442-0418
ofa@ofa.org
(Hip registry)

Activity Clubs

Write to the following organizations for information on the activities they sponsor.

American Kennel Club (AKC)
260 Madison Avenue, 4th Floor
New York, NY 10016
(212) 696-8200
www.akc.org
(Conformation Shows, Obedience Trials, Field Trials and Hunting Tests, Agility, Canine Good Citizen, Lure Coursing, Herding, Tracking, Earthdog Tests, Coonhunting)

United Kennel Club (UKC)
100 East Kilgore Road
Portage, MI 49002-5584
(616) 343-9020
www.ukcdogs.com
(Conformation Shows, Obedience Trials, Agility, Hunting for Various Breeds, Terrier Trials and more)

North American Flyball Association
1400 West Devon Avenue, #152
Chicago, IL 60660
www.flyball.org

Trainers

Association of Pet Dog Trainers
66 Morris Avenue, Suite 2A
Springfield, NJ 07081
(800) PET-DOGS
www.apdp.com

National Association of Dog Obedience Instructors
2286 East Steel Road
St. Johns, MI 48879
www.nadoi.org

Dog Friendly Web Sites

The following Web sites offer a variety of experiences for the dog-loving Internet surfer. Some sites present specific breed information, while others provide quizzes and question-naires to help you decide which dog breed is the best one for you and your family. You can view photographs, research breeders and rescue organizations in your area, find out the best ways to exercise or travel with your pet or just discover more about *canis familiaris*. Enjoy!

Dog Breed Information Center
www.dogbreedinfo.com
This is a well-designed site with cute doggie graphics and easy-to-use links. Log on to donate toys to rescue organiza-tions, post messages for like-minded dog folk, take question-naires to discover which dog breed is best suited to your family and your home, view a plethora of canine photographs or discover the answers to frequently asked dog-care and -training questions.

Choosing the Perfect Dog
www.choosingtheperfectdog.net
Another good, all-purpose site for dog owners or dog-owner wannabes. Information is presented in a very organized man-ner, with helpful sidebars and links. Practical answers are given to questions such as "How do I match a dog to my lifestyle?" Or "How much time/money/stuff do I need to provide for a dog?" The site prompts visitors to think carefully about getting a dog, and to responsibly research dog breeds so that everyone involved lives happily ever after.

Good News for Pets
www.goodnewsforpets.com
This weekly digest provides interesting tidbits on all things canine related. It profiles people who are active in the dog community, provides nutrition facts, addresses legal issues

Beyond the
Basics

and focuses attention on how dogs are portrayed in books and on film. Visit every Monday for the "Pet Question of the Week."

Dog Advisors
www.dogadvisors.com

This is a fun site where the fancier can delve a little deeper and learn a little more about his or her favorite dog breeds. Different breeds are highlighted at various times, as are specific breeders.

United States Dog Agility Association, Inc. (USDAA)
www.usdaa.com

This USDAA is an international site that gives visitors the opportunity to find out the latest news in the world of agility training. It provides an events calendar, records titles and tournaments, defines performance standards and lists affiliated groups. "Front Page News" is updated on a weekly basis.

Canine Freestyle Federation, Inc.
www.canine-freestyle.org

Welcome to the world of Canine Freestyle—or doggie dancing, if you will. Canine freestyle is performed by dog and trainer in a ring, and all moves are choreographed to music. To learn more, visit this well-designed, comprehensive Web site. The CFF also maintains records of freestyle events and publishes a newsletter.

Pets Welcome
www.petswelcome.com

If you plan on travelling with your pet, a visit to this site is a must. The listings page offers information on over 25,000 hotels, bed & breakfasts, ski resorts, campgrounds and pet-friendly beaches. Plenty of advice and knowledge are provided for those who can't imagine leaving their pet at home.

Vet Info.com
www.vetinfo.com

If your dog is suffering from a particular ailment, you can find out more about it by visiting vetinfo.com. The format of this site is easy to use, with each disease listed in alphabetical order. To delve even deeper into your pet's health, you might subscribe to *Vetinfo Digest* for its "Ask Dr. Mike" Segment.

Printed in the USA
CPSIA information can be obtained
at www.ICGtesting.com
JSHW012011140824
68134JS00023B/2358